A Sympathetic Understanding
of the Child

Birth to Sixteen

David Elkind
University of Rochester

SECOND EDITION

A Sympathetic Understanding of the Child

Birth to Sixteen

Allyn and Bacon, Inc.
Boston, London, Sydney

Second printing . . . September, 1978

Copyright © 1978 and 1974 by Allyn and Bacon, Inc.
470 Atlantic Avenue, Boston, Massachusetts 02210

Portions of this book first appeared in *A Sympathetic
Understanding of the Child: Six to Sixteen,* copyright ©
1971 by Allyn and Bacon, Inc.

Library of Congress Cataloging in Publication Data

Elkind, David, 1931-
    A sympathetic understanding of the child, birth to 16.

    Bibliography: p.
    Includes index.
    1. Child psychology.   2. Adolescent psychology.
I. Title.

BF721.E366 1978   649'.1'019   77-16150
ISBN 0-205-06016 (*hardbound*)
ISBN 0-205-06015-3 (*softbound*)

Contents

Preface to the Second Edition

This second edition of *A Sympathetic Understanding of the Child: Birth to Sixteen* was motivated largely by the reaction of readers. The major objection to the book has come from students who disliked the discussion of boy-girl differences and the pervasive use of "he" in talking about the child. In rereading the book I discovered that the criticisms were well taken. Accordingly, the revision is devoted to the elimination, wherever possible, of unthinking sex-role stereotyping and the uniform use of "he" when speaking of the child and also to some updating of content.

I found that eliminating the sex-role stereotyping was somewhat easier than dealing with pronominal usage. The alternatives in this regard are not very attractive to a writer. I find both the exclusive use of the plural or of "he and she" rather awkward. What I decided to do instead was simply to alternate the use of he and she. For example, I speak of "he" in the descriptive chapters on infancy and middle childhood and of "she" in the chapters on early childhood and adolescence. The use of "he" and "she" is also alternated in the age profiles. Girls are even, boys are odd (years).

This is far from a perfect solution because the shift from he to she can be jarring. On the other hand, I believe that it has some special fringe benefits. The exclusive use of she to describe some age groups occasionally produces a "shock of recognition," a recognition of how our language does indeed stereotype the sexes. I very much hope that the way in which I have chosen to deal with sexism in our writing and in our portrayals of children will satisfy those who found the earlier edition offensive.

Please understand, however, that I in no way wish to contend that there are no sex differences in psychological traits and abilities. Unfortunately our treatment of women resembles our treatment of children in this regard. We treat children as if they were most like us in their thoughts and least like us in their feelings. In fact, of course, just the reverse is true. And women are treated as if they were most like men in our weaknesses, least like men in our strengths. Again, just the reverse is true. Women are most like men in their strengths (intelligence, motivation, commitment) and least like men in their weaknesses (physical in the case of women, psychological in the case of men).

So, in trying to remove the sex-role stereotyping and the sexist language from this book, I in no way want to minimize the very real differences between men and women. What I do hope we can move toward is a realistic appraisal of those differences that is based on fact rather than fancy. Adults and children, men and women, will engage in the most productive interaction when these interactions are founded on real, rather than imagined, differences between the sexes.

Introduction to
A Sympathetic
Understanding of the Child
Six to Sixteen

Every book has a history. The impetus for this book came from an attempt to provide a brief survey course of child development to "lay" teachers, those without formal training in child psychology and education. What was needed, it seemed, was a presentation of salient facts about the emotional, intellectual, and social development of children in nontechnical language and in a nontechnical format. The chapters in this book are the distillation of that brief survey course.

In part, the ages from six to sixteen were chosen because they are the crucial school years. During this period the child acquires the basic tool skills of reading, writing, and arithmetic, as well as the fundaments of science, language, and social studies. It is, consequently, the period during which basic attitudes towards academic endeavors are formed and the child's concept of himself as a good or poor student emerges. School success and failure play an important part in determining both the value the growing person places upon intellectual activities generally and his own mental abilities in particular. Then too, the era from six to sixteen is also the period of assimilation to the peer cultures and to other social institutions, such as the church.

The age period from six to sixteen is unique in other ways as well. The age of six marks the entrance into childhood proper and the first exposure to formal education, while the age of sixteen marks the end of early adolescence and is the way station to late adolescence and adulthood. In some respects, the orientation of the young adolescent is closer to that of the child than to the older adolescent and adult. In short, while all "age cuts" are necessarily arbitrary, the cut from six to sixteen can be justified on educational, psychological, and social grounds.

Still another general comment about the content is in order. As the text makes clear, the material is based upon research and observation of predominantly white, middle-class children. The reason for this is that up until a few years ago, most psychological research with children involved mainly middle-class children. To be sure, there is a sense in which the old saw "Children are children" is true, namely, the sense that certain growth trends and patterns hold for all children. In another sense, however, the saying is clearly false. Children do differ in such things as language, values, attitudes, and manners according to the social and economic milieu in which they are raised. This book attempts to suggest the influence of these factors on various aspects of child behavior, but no systematic treatment of the effects of social, economic, and ethnic variations on the actions and thoughts of children is presented.

With these limitations in mind, we can turn to the major purpose of the introduction, which is to discuss the matter of observing children. As the title of this book indicates, its aim is to provide a "sympathetic understanding" of children. While the book tries to present the world from the child's perspective, appreciation of the material will be greatly enhanced if the reader has occasion to observe children at first hand, particularly in the classroom. Effective observation is an art that can be learned even by those who are not naturally talented in this regard.

The natural observation of children is one of the teacher's most indispensable tools. Such observation can be used to provide information at three different levels of generality. At the most general level, natural observation can provide many valuable insights about how the children function as a group and about the group's unique qualities and characteristics. A second function of natural observation is to help teachers recognize particular roles that characterize every group and that are to some extent independent of the particular child who fills the role at any given time. While there is always danger in categorizing children, such categorization is useful in providing (among other things) guidelines for handling problem children. Finally, natural observation can be employed to observe the individual child in all of his uniqueness. Now let us look at these three types of observation in a little more detail.

Observing Classroom Groups

The classroom group is a true group in the sense that it meets regularly in a particular place to perform particular functions.

One way to observe such groups is from the standpoint of their effectiveness in achieving the goal for which they are constituted, namely, learning. In observing a group we might ask then what features of group interaction support or interfere with the major group function of learning.

When classroom groups are observed from this perspective, several types of groups can be distinguished. First there is the *cohesive*, or *supportive*, group, wherein individual members have high positive regard for other members. That is to say, when one child is successful, other children in the group are likely to be pleased and complimentary. Contrariwise, when a child in the cohesive group fails, the children are supportive and nonderogatory. There is a spirit of helpfulness and good humor during group activities and an air of quiet activity when individual work is in progress. In coherent groups one finds children who have close friends but who also remain friendly with other children within the group.

A second identifiable type of classroom group might be called *fragmented*. In such groups there are usually several subgroups, or cliques, that are more or less antagonistic to one another. (In some cases a subgroup may even mean a single child who has been isolated from all of the other subgroups.) There is often considerable friction between the various factions in the fragmented classroom. Friction is often apparent in the hostility shown by the members of one group to a successful member of a different subgroup and by the gleeful gloating when a member of another subgroup is unsuccessful. This hostility between subgroups often interferes with activities carried on by the group as a whole. Likewise, there are apt to be more instances of children disturbing other children when youngsters are working alone at their desks.

A third type of group that can be observed in the classroom might be called the *disorganized*, or *chaotic*, group. In such constellations, subgroups are loosely organized, and children move from one subgroup to another. There is little concern for academic success or failure. Behaviors that are supported by the group are disruptive. In effect, children who are loud, noisy, or funny are supported by the group, while those who are quiet and obedient are likely to be teased and derogated. There is no real spirit of helpfulness within the group but rather one of emotional contagion—the emotional charge of one child seems to ignite similar charges in the other children. In a manner of speaking, there is a kind of emotional chain reaction that gives the group its chaotic spirit.

The above-mentioned categories in no way exhaust the ways in which classroom groups can be described. Another equally valuable way of looking at groups is from the standpoint of the role played by the teacher. To illustrate, some groups might be described as *democratic* when teacher and children share in the decision-making process. Other groups might be called *autocratic* when children play little or no role in the decision-making process. Finally, in *laissez-faire* groups the teacher exercises little or no control, and the group lacks unified direction. In observing groups, therefore, it is well to look at them from several different standpoints. In theory, of course, the cohesive, democratic group should be the most effective in attaining its educational goals. In practice, however, even the cohesive democratic group can be chaotic on occasion just as the fragmented group will sometimes display cohesion. Descriptive categories are always relative and never absolute.

Observing Pupil Roles

Within any classroom group, particular children gradually assume certain roles that are characteristic of the classroom group in general and that may differ considerably from the child's role in other situations. Indeed, while the child's personality is an important factor in the determination of the role he plays in the group, it is not the whole story. In different groups, the same role can be taken by individuals with quite different personality styles. For example, men of many different personality types have held the role of President of the United States. In the classroom, as in other groups, roles are defined by the group, and someone is required to fill each role. Let us look now at some of the more common group-originated roles.

Perhaps the most universal classroom role is that of the clown, whose job is to make faces, pull pranks, and in general, keep the class amused. A related role is that of the class "fool," who becomes the butt of jokes and teasing because he is clumsy and slow. The two roles are sometimes combined so that the same child may play both roles. Indeed, the clever fool's best defense is often to become the deliberate clown. At the other extreme are the class "idols"—children who are handsomely endowed physically, intellectually, and, usually, financially. These are the children who "have everything" and who are admired and envied by their classmates.

Other notable roles within the classroom are those of the "athlete"; the "brain," or "scholar"; the "sissy," or "coward"; the "bully"; the "ugly duckling"; the "dummy"; and the "promoter," or "entrepreneur." Among girls one finds "teacher's pet," the "stuck-up," the "tomboy," the "boy-crazy," and the "siren" as well as the "little lady." While not every group has children who fill all of these roles, at least some of them are prominent in most children's groups. Indeed, one sees the same roles being played by high school and college students. It is as if the group needs to have various personality traits and qualities exemplified in particular individuals.

In looking at a group from the point of view of the roles played by its members, it is helpful to see what roles are emphasized or de-emphasized by the group. The attitudes of the children towards those who fill particular roles is of particular interest. It says something important about the group if children laugh *at* rather than *with* the clown. Likewise, if the group idols are not particularly "nice" children, it says something of interest about the group's general attitudes and values. Information about the roles emphasized by the group and the qualities of the people who fill them, together with the group's attitudes towards the roles, provide an overall impression of the group's unique spirit and quality.

Observing the Individual Child

Ideally, the individual child should be observed in the context of case history data about his home, family, health, and any traumatic experiences he has undergone. Even without case history data, however, much can be gleaned from natural observation of the child in the classroom. The technique is to focus upon a particular child and to take a sort of Sherlock Holmes attitude towards him. That is to say, by looking for telltale clues provided by the child, one can try to guess what is going on within him and speculate about his home, family, and personal history.

Natural observation of the individual child in the classroom could well begin with the most obvious thing, namely, appearance. Is the child of average height and weight for his age?

If not, in what directions are the deviations? If the child is taller or smaller than his peers or if he is noticeably thinner or fatter, we can immediately guess at some aspects of his experience. The large child is likely to be treated as older and stronger, while the small child is likely to be treated as somewhat younger. The thin child is likely to be bullied, and the fat child is likely to be teased. Similar guesses can be made on the basis of whether the child is attractive or unattractive. Another aspect of appearance to be noted is the child's clothing. Children who dress differently from their peers are likely to be teased, whereas children who are nicely dressed are likely to be admired and envied. Other aspects of appearance could be mentioned, but these should suffice to illustrate the kinds of inferences that can be made.

After the child's appearance has been noted, aspects of his behavior can be observed. Is the child impulsive and easily frustrated or is he calm and unflappable even under stress? Is he outgoing and happy, or shy and withdrawn? Does he relate better to boys, to girls, or to adults? Is he well mannered or boorish? Is he sensitive or insensitive to the feelings and needs of others? How do other children and adults respond to him? Do they like him or dislike him? What makes him attractive to others or puts them off? What is the nature of his speech? Is it loud, soft, or in between? From these features of the child's behavior one can get a fair description of the child.

Such a description can be the starting point for speculation. One might, for example, assume that the shy, withdrawn child has a poor self-image and is lacking in self-confidence and that positive signs of acceptance by the group might help to bring him out of his shell. Likewise, the child who appears to be boorish and insensitive to other children may simply be frightened and behave that way out of fear. If such a child is given group support for his achievements, he may move out of his egocentrism. These are but a few of the examples of how careful classroom observation of the individual child can lead to inferences as to what might be done to integrate the child better within the classroom group and to further his learning activity.

In summary, there is a wealth of observational materials in the classroom. Children can be observed at the level of the group as a group, at the level of roles taken by children within the group, and at the level of the individual child. The categories and questions given above are merely starting points for observation. While it is well to have questions that guide observation, it is also well to leave oneself open for the new and the unexpected. Not all behavior will fall into ready-made categories, and it is sometimes more meaningful to introduce a new category than to force the behaviors into a category that is inappropriate.

As the above discussion of classroom observation suggests, there is more to such observation than one might guess at first glance. Indeed, there is more to developing a sympathetic understanding of children than merely reading about them. While such reading is helpful, as we hope the present book will be, a better appreciation of the child's world will come if the reader makes an effort to observe children and to think about the observations in the context of the descriptions given here. Hopefully, this book will convey how much there is to know about children. And the more we know about children, the more we know about ourselves. Perhaps that is one reason why the study of children is so endlessly fascinating.

Introduction

In the introduction to *A Sympathetic Understanding of the Child: Six to Sixteen,* I began with the observation that every book has a history in the sense that it grows out of the author's personal background and experience. After a book has been in print, however, it also acquires a past of its own, a past that grows out of the experience of those who have read and used the book. One of the comments I have heard most often about the book is that I left out a very important period, namely, the first five years of life. The early years were omitted in the first book because it was originally meant as a supplement for elementary school teachers. It turns out, however, that the book has been used with many groups for whom a discussion of the first five years of life would also be instructive. Hence, this second book covers the period from birth to sixteen.

In treating the first five years of life, I have tried to stay with the same format I used in the child and adolescent sections. Again the reader will find sections on physical and mental development, as well as sections dealing with the child in various social contexts. Included, also, are brief age profiles wherein I have summarized and modified, whenever necessary because of contemporary research findings, the age-wise descriptions of development offered by Gesell.

Before closing this introduction, I should say something about my biases insofar as early childhood and early childhood education are concerned. The amount of research done on and the number of programs developed for infants and young children over the past decade has been tremendous, but the results are far from clear-cut and unambiguous. My position on the appropriate education for young children is based on my reading of the research literature, on my discussions with early childhood educators in all parts of the country, and upon my own research and clinical work with young children. I believe that it is our major responsibility and task, as parents and educators, to establish within the child, during the preschool years, a strong sense of autonomy, initiative, self-confidence, and self-esteem. I hope that the description of the first years of life will help parents and teachers better evaluate which practices and attitudes are most conducive to the child's attainment of a healthy sense of himself as a competent and worthy person.

A Note
to Parents
and Teachers

Raising children is not an easy task, and most parents (even child psychologists like myself) are a little defensive about their child-rearing practices. All of us are aware that we have made mistakes, have been unduly harsh at times, and have gone overboard to atone for these excesses. While we should always try to do better, we need to accept the fact that our failures are very human failures and in no way indicate that we are evil people or bad parents. No one has, or ever will have, all the answers to interpersonal difficulties. So long as the majority of the child's experiences are positive, he can cope very well with occasional parental mistakes.

Parents also differ tremendously in their personal styles of child-rearing. There are no absolutes in this field. What works for one parent will be a total disaster for another. Parents and children differ so much, both within the same family and between families, that each parent-child relation is unique. I recall seeing a father harshly chastise his daughter in the supermarket. I was quick to mentally criticize him, but as I stood behind him and his child at the checkout counter, and saw the daughter nuzzle up to her father, I sensed the love underneath the harshness in his voice. His daughter knew that this was his way of communicating love and acceptance.

That doesn't mean, of course, that love and acceptance will solve all child-rearing problems, although it helps. Some children seem bent on destroying the love and attention the most concerned and devoted parents lavish upon them, while some children seem devoted to parents who are self-centered and rejecting of their children. It is simply not fair to blame parents when a child presents problems, because those problems can arise from a host of factors, such as birth order, intellectual ability, or temperament, that are relatively independent of parental influence. Some problem children have problem parents, but that is not always, or necessarily, the case.

What I am saying is that the vast majority of parents want to be good parents and to do the right things for their children. This impression comes from years of working with teacher and parent groups in all parts of this country. Certainly many of us fail in our efforts and for many different reasons, but that doesn't necessarily make us bad parents or bad people. Most of us do a pretty good job despite the many societal changes in values and sex roles that are affecting family integration, and which make child rearing more challenging. While this is no reason for complacency, it is a reason for feeling good about ourselves as parents and for continuing to do the best job we can in rearing our children.

The same holds true for teachers. Most teachers work very hard, and try to do a good job, and they succeed. The men who sent spaceships to the moon were educated in American public schools. Surely, American education can be improved and changed, but that could be said of any institution. Unfortunately, teachers often feel that they must succeed with every child or else they have failed. This is a human feeling, with which every physician, and every psychotherapist, and indeed all professionals, must contend. It is the feeling that we are more than human and can succeed in every case. The best of us are only human, and no teacher, no more than any professional, succeeds with everyone. Therefore, we have to remain content with the assurance that we are doing a good job and are helpful to some, if not all, of those persons to whom we minister.

Again, however, this should not be viewed as an argument for complacency. Good teaching, like good parenting, is hard work. There are simply no shortcuts, no easy ways, to helping children grow and develop into independent, self-confident, and responsible adults. One has to continue to work at being a good parent, just as one has to continue to work at being a good wife or husband. Such work carries its own rewards in that it helps us to keep growing and realizing ourselves as individuals.

A Sympathetic Understanding of the Child

Birth to Sixteen

PART I

The Infant and the Young Child

1 Personal and Social Development in the Infant

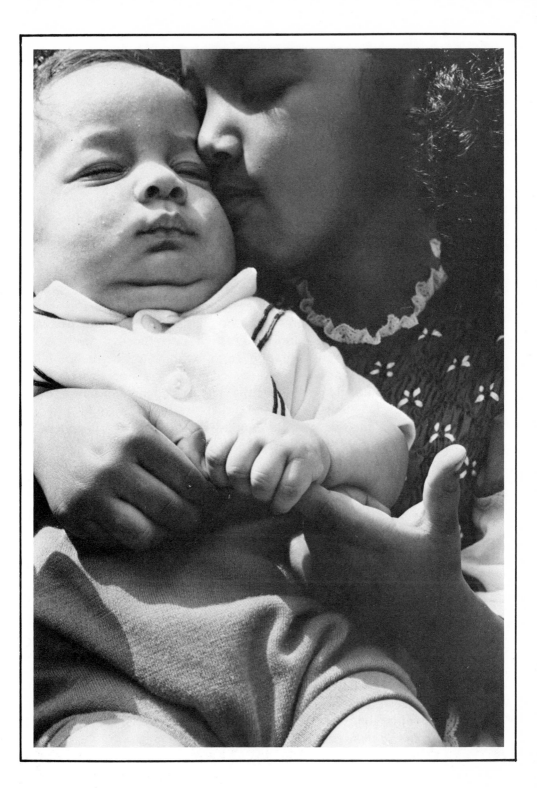

The infancy period, roughly the first two years of life, is certainly one of the most remarkable and significant eras in the whole life cycle. Within two short years, a squalling, uncoordinated bundle of wants is transformed into a walking, talking individual with strong social attachments and a will of his own. To be sure, the two-year-old has a long way to go before maturity, but the transformation—the enormous "leap" across that boundary that separates the infant who only can use expressive cries and gestures from the child who can use an arbitrary, socially derived symbol system—has been successfully made.

The transformation from infancy to toddlerhood has other facets as well. Towards the end of the second year of life, the toddler gives evidence that he has a concept of himself that, to some extent, guides and directs his behavior. In his prideful "noes" the two-year-old demonstrates that he is a person to be reckoned with. It is this sense of a separate self, which affects all of his relationships with others, that helps make the social interactions of the two-year-old qualitatively different from the social interchanges of the infant.

If human infancy is a period of remarkable accomplishments, it is also a period of extreme vulnerability. The newborn infant is exposed, for the first time, to a totally new environment where he is susceptible to a variety of diseases for which he has, after a period of immunity, to build up new defenses. He is vulnerable, too, because he cannot care for himself and must depend upon the ministrations of others for the satisfaction of all of his needs. Even more importantly, the infant is socially vulnerable; without the necessary minimum of love and physical mothering, the delicate, budding sense of self-worth and trust in others can be badly damaged. The price of the remarkable transformations that occur in infancy is, thus, the extreme vulnerability of the infant to vagaries of the biological, physical, and social worlds.

"You forget how small they are" is a comment the mothers of young infants hear again and again from parents whose offspring are full-grown, or at least half-grown. Infants are indeed small; the average infant at birth has a head-to-feet length of about 20 inches and he weighs about 7.5 pounds. The body proportions of an infant are far different than they will be at a later date, and the length of his head is about a fourth the length of his body. His head, moreover, has about the same circumference as his chest, and his arms and legs are quite short. To get some idea of the problems these proportions impose on a young infant, the reader has only to imagine his or her problems if your head were the size of a large beach ball while the rest of you remained the same size.

Although the infant makes tremendous progress during the first two years of life, he does not start from a zero baseline. At birth, the infant has a number of operative reflexes, such as the "startle" pattern that can be elicited by sudden sharp sounds, and the sucking reflex that can be induced by stroking the infant's lips. Newborn infants also exhibit a grasp reflex, which is strong enough so that if the infant takes hold of an adult's fingers, the adult can actually lift the infant from the crib on the strength of his reflex.

In addition to reflexes, the young infant also has some sensory abilities at his disposal soon after birth. He can discriminate among loud, sudden, and other sounds and he can distinguish between sweet and bitter water solutions. Visually, even the young infant shows a preference for more complex patterns, such as newsprint, over "less interesting" patterns, such as lines. Likewise, while the infant's vocal apparatus is relatively undeveloped, he can emit a variety of sounds (crying and cooing) that clearly portray his emotional states.

As the infant develops over the first two years, maturation takes several characteristic directions. In general, growth is from the "head" to the "tail" and the infant acquires motor control over his head before he acquires comparable control over his arms, which in turn appears before he develops good motor control over his legs. Growth also progresses from the center of the body towards the outside or periphery. A child will be able to flail his arms before he can oppose his thumb and his forefinger, and, in the same way, a child will learn how to walk before he will learn how to curl his toes.

Sociocultural Change

Child-rearing practices during the infancy period, such as the age at which children are toilet trained, are very much affected by the sociocultural era in which a child is reared. Less than a century ago, parents were urged to toilet train their children early (by three or four months) and to sew up the sleeves of children's nightclothes so that they could not touch their genitals or suck their thumbs. Likewise, breast-feeding has at various times been strongly advocated or dismissed as unnecessary. Indeed, fashions in child-rearing are more in evidence and more changeable during the infancy period than at any other developmental epoch.

Fortunately, fashions in child-rearing have not been entirely arbitrary and show definite directions. Since the beginning of this century, for example, the trend has been away from a moralistic approach to child behavior. Young children are no longer regarded as invested with "original sin" manifested in such behavior as masturbation and "willfulness." Thanks to the work of Freud and of Gesell, it has come to be recognized that many infant behaviors, such as interest in the genitals, is common to all children and is a natural phase of child growth.

Another finding in the evolution of ideas about child-rearing is that there are no absolute and final answers to such questions as whether or not to breast-feed. If the mother wishes to breast-feed her infant, then this will have beneficial effects, in part, because the mother will use the feeding period to fondle and caress her offspring. On the other hand, if a mother, for whatever reason, does not want to breast-feed her infant, she probably should not do so. If she does breast-feed out of a feeling of obligation, her reluctance will be communicated to the infant with untoward effects. This is true because a mother who breast-feeds unwillingly will communicate two different messages, one of acceptance and another of rejection, which will confuse and disturb the infant. In short, whether or not the mother breast-feeds the infant is less important for his well-being than her display of a positive attitude towards him.

One of the most significant changes in our conception of child-rearing is the recognition that the biological mother need not be the prime caretaker during the first few years of life. Until recently it was generally believed, at least among middle-class mothers, that the child would suffer unless cared for full time by its own mother. Perhaps to justify this belief, a strong conviction arose to the effect that is was "natural" for a mother to "want" to be with her children during the formative years. Clearly, the implication ran, mothers who do not want to care for their young children are "unnatural."

Attitudes such as these are changing very rapidly, however, and the causes are multiple and complex. On the one hand, a great deal of research on children reared by nonbiological mothers in Israel, in Russia, and in America gave evidence that children reared by mother surrogates suffered no untoward effects as a result. This conclusion should have been obvious from the fact that for centuries the children of the wealthy in America, as in Europe, have been reared by mother surrogates, such as the renowned "nanny." It was, however, the women's liberation movement that brought these findings and observations to the fore and made it obvious that there was no necessity for mothers to stay home with their young children so long as adequate day-care facilities were available, and so long as the mother spent some time each day with her child.

While it is recognized today that the infant does not need the full-time ministrations of his biological mother, the importance of adequate "mothering" for healthy development seems well established. An infant needs a certain basic amount of being held, fondled, rocked, and talked to during the formative years for normal growth and development. If he is deprived of such mothering, and of adequate nutrition, and environmental stimulation as well, he can develop severe emotional problems or at least not realize his full potential for competence.

What we see today, then, is an important distinction between the infant's *need* for mothering, which is well established, and the mythology about *who* must do the mothering. Today, middle-class mothers are coming to recognize that their having little inclination to be with their young children all day long is no reflection on their femininity, nor will it have un-toward effects upon the infant so long as he is adequately cared for by someone, and so long as the mother spends at least a couple of hours with the infant each day. Indeed, a mother who comes home from school or work to enjoy her child for a few hours may be better for him than the unhappy, frustrated mother who spends the whole day at home with her child out of some mistaken belief that she is the only one who can ade-quately feed, clothe, and change her baby.

Sociocultural change is affecting the role of the father as well as that of the mother. Many young fathers today, for exam-ple, wish to be present during the birth of their children. These fathers take a greater share of responsibility for feeding, changing, and bathing the baby than was probably true for their own fathers. Such patterns, while far from being universal, reflect the breakdown of rigid sex-role behaviors, which is also exemplified in such things as the long hair worn by men and by unisex modes of dress. In contrast to parental practice of a few decades ago, today's father is likely to be as involved in infant care as the mother. Moreover, he is likely to enjoy it and not feel that his feeding or changing the baby is in any way a reflection on his masculinity.

General Characteristics of the Infancy Period

Perhaps the major characteristics of the infancy period are the young child's relative dependence and helplessness. Despite the gigantic strides made in two years, a child even at age two would be unable to fend for himself in the world. The depen-dency and helplessness of the infant have both positive and negative consequences.

The smallness, the needfulness, and the dependency of the infant call out protective and loving impulses on the part of parents and other adults. Because infants cause little damage, do not challenge adult authority, or make outrageous demands, they tend to be enjoyed and catered to. Furthermore, all babies are "cute" and their behavior is universally accepted by adults. Consequently, a parent is likely to get positive comments about the baby from whoever sees him. As children get older, other adults become more critical and less accepting than they were of infants, and parents are, of necessity, a little more defensive.

The negative aspect of the infant's dependence and help-lessness is that this combination of traits sometimes runs afoul of particular parents. In recent years, the "battered child" syndrome has come to be recognized as being quite prevalent. Battered infants have usually been hit, dropped, or slammed against a wall by one or another of the parents who "could not stand" the crying or some other aspect of infant behavior. While all parents sometimes get angry at their children and even have destructive fantasies about their offspring, it takes a truly troubled parent actually to assault an infant. In some cases, the child is not hit but isolated in a cold garage (where he may catch pneumonia) or tied to a chair or crib. The parents who per-petrate such acts are disturbed people, in whom the help-lessness of the infant seems to provoke uncontrollable anger. Such parents are often found to be individuals who have never been able to accept fully their own dependency needs and who hate in their children what they most hate in themselves.

While dependency and helplessness are clearly major aspects of the infancy period, it is necessary to stress the other side of the picture as well. Infants take the initiative in many activities, such as "babbling" and other forms of play, that they use to promote their own linguistic and cognitive growth. Children also initiate a variety of social contacts as well, and smile and coo at parents to catch their attention. In other words, while dependency and helplessness in an adult are usually as-sociated with a passive attitude towards life, this is not true for the infant. However dependent or helpless he is, the infant is an active participant in the sociopsychological world in which he lives and grows.

The World of Self, Home, and Community

During the first year or two of life, a very basic component of the child's self-concept is elaborated: the notion of the self as "object." At birth, the young infant does not clearly distinguish between himself and the outer world. He does not distinguish, for example, between sensations that come from within or outside himself. If something touches his skin that he does not like, he cries but does not try to move the thing away. Likewise, the young infant has no notion that objects are permanent or real and continue to exist when he is not looking at them. If you play with an infant and then duck out of sight he does not cry, because for him, out of sight is literally out of mind.

Towards the end of the first year of life, however, the infant gradually constructs a world of objects that he believes exist even when he is not looking at them. For example, a ten-month-old infant will cry when his mother leaves the room, whereas he would not have done so a few short months earlier. The reason is that the infant now has an inner representation or picture of the mother that can stand for her in her absence.

Just as the infant gradually constructs a representation of objects outside himself, so does he also begin to build a notion of himself as an object in a particular place. One evidence of the new concept of the self as object is the fear of strangers manifested by many young infants towards the end of the first year and into the second. The infant's fear of strangers reflects not only the ability to discriminate between familiar and unfamiliar faces but also the first apprehension of danger to the self. The child will show fear only when he has a concept of himself as an object that can be hurt or destroyed. The concept of self as object is the fundament upon which all later components of the self-concept are built and about which they are all organized.

Within the home, the impact of the parents on the child's concept of self as object depends upon the nature of the family structure. If the infant is a first child, parents may be overly cautious and fearful in their treatment of him. If he is a later child, parents will be more experienced and relaxed about things like bathing and changing him. Likewise, they will be more calm when he has a fever or shows other signs of distress, since they will have been through the whole sequence before. The tenseness and "high-strungness" one often finds in first children may relate, in part at least, to the nervousness of parents regarding their firstborn. Firstborn children may acquire a certain insecurity in relation to the self that was communicated by parental tensions.

To other siblings in the home, a baby often comes as something of a threat. The infant captures the attention of both the parents and friends and relatives who visit. The older child often feels slighted and left out. Particularly pernicious are un-thinking comments about the baby's "cuteness" and how he is going to be much handsomer than his brother (prettier than her sister). Such comments are not well received by little people. It is not surprising, then, that many older children occasionally attack their infant siblings and try to make their lives miserable.

Perhaps the best way to minimize such sibling rivalry is to prepare well in advance for the baby's coming, particularly by discussing what he will look like and what his name will be. If the older sibling is allowed to help in the preparations and to have specific jobs he can do to help, he will feel a part of the event. It is important, too, to reassure the older child that he is loved and wanted. Although parents may feel that this is obvious and unnecessary, they can often save themselves much grief if they verbalize their love for the older child and how much he means to them. Parents need to verbalize their love be-cause children often assume that they are not loved and badly need reassurance that they are. In that respect, they are really not different from adults who also like to *hear* that they are loved.

Driving with my son Bobby one day, I reached over to touch him and said, "Bobby, I love you; do you know that?" He replied, "No." Surprised, I asked, "How come?" to which he re-sponded, "You never told me before." Even child psychologists need to be reminded to verbalize their positive feelings.

Until recently, the community had little responsibility for, or interest in, infant care. With the exception of care for unwed mothers, and the provision of adoption personnel, the community was relatively impervious to problems of rearing infants. With the civil rights movement, the concern for dis-advantaged children, and the liberation of women, however, communities are increasingly recognizing the need for com-munity sponsored programs for infants and young children. It seems inevitable that day-care programs supported in part by government funds will eventually be widespread across the country.

The provision of large-scale day-care programs for infants and young children holds much promise but also poses many problems. Such programs will surely free many women from having to stay home with young children and allow them to pursue their own careers. Children are likely to benefit if the facilities are good and if they enjoy the space, toys, and companionship they might not have had at home. One of the problems is to get a sufficient number of adequately trained people to work in such centers. Some of the current programs aimed at training nonprofessionals may help solve the problem. Nonetheless, getting sufficient numbers of people who are emotionally sound as well as adequately prepared to deal with young children is probably the single biggest obstacle to the successful implementation of large-scale day-care programs.

Choosing a Day-Care Center for Your Child

It is important to choose a good day-care setting for your child, and the following suggestions may help in making that choice. Day-care centers are usually listed in the Yellow Pages. Most parents will want one that is conveniently located. After finding the centers that make good demographic sense, it is useful to check with the local fire and health officers to see whether the schools have met the minimum safety and health codes of the community. In some states, licensing of day-care centers and directors is required and only licensed centers should be considered.

The next step is a visit to the center itself. You will want to investigate the location of the center and see whether there is easy access to play and toilet areas, whether there is sufficient large- and small-muscle play equipment of good quality to satisfy the needs of the group, and whether the setting is light and dry. Next you need to inquire into the director's background and into the training and background of the teachers and aides. Ideally, the director and teachers should have academic degrees in early childhood education. At the very least, there should be one supervisory person at the setting who has such training.

Another important aspect of the center about which you want to inquire is the child-to-teacher ratio. For two-year-old children, a ratio of four to one is optimum. By the time children are three to four, a ratio of from eight or ten to one is workable. Settings in which the pupil-to-teacher ratio is very high should probably be avoided. High ratios mean that young children will not get the individual attention and supervision they need for the day-care center to be a really valuable experience.

Once you have decided on a center (and it is good to check with friends and neighbors regarding your choice as a kind of validation by consensus), you need to prepare your child for the experience. In general, the younger the child, the more preparation is required. Preparation involves visiting the school with your child, introducing him to the teachers, and allowing him to play with some of the equipment. Several trips of this kind will familiarize the child with the setting and the people. In addition, you need to talk to the child about the school, about the fact that he is going to be there for a while every day, and to tell him that you will take him and bring him back. It is important to emphasize taking him to school and fetching him back rather than the "leaving" him at the school. Most children who have had prior experience with baby-sitters adapt well to the day-care setting.

Parents should expect certain consequences as a result of their child's enrollment in a day-care setting. First, your child is more likely to catch colds and other communicable diseases because of his greater exposure. He may also develop immunities earlier. Fights and other unhappinesses are to be expected when young children are together for long periods of time. Your child may also become quite attached to a teacher or an aide, but this is healthy and in no way means that the child no longer cares for his parents. Children, no less than adults, can care for more than one person at a time.

So far I haven't said anything about the type of program offered by the school. This is because, or so it seems to me, most good programs for young children will have many components in common. Therefore, the major things to look for are a safe, attractive physical plant and well-trained, warm, and competent teachers in a setting where there is a low child-to-teacher ratio. In such a setting, the child is bound to get a rich educational as well as social-emotional experience.

Infant-Adult Relationships

We have already spoken of some aspects of infant-adult relationships in the discussion of the infant's dependency and helplessness. There are, however, some additional aspects of the infant-adult relation that require comment. First of all, there is the establishment, early in infancy, of a true sense of interpersonal relations. Many mothers report that they really come to see their infants as persons only after they manage to establish eye contact. This usually does not happen until an infant is about a month old. This eye contact seems to promote a peculiar "chemistry" that makes the mother feel she is relating and communicating to another individual. Once eye contact is established, child-rearing takes on a qualitatively different tone.

Another aspect of infant-adult relations that has recently come to the fore concerns individual differences that seem to have a genetic component. Some investigators have found that soon after birth children can be grouped with regard to their ability to adapt to new and changing situations. The majority of children adapt to new situations with relative ease, while a small minority are upset every time they are confronted with a new challenge in the environment.

Apparently, these individual differences in adaptability are quite long-lived, and persist well into childhood and adolescence. When children who have difficulty adapting are recognized early, a number of things can be done to make their lives easier. Most important is counseling parents not to expect too much and not to demand too much of these youngsters all at once. When parents recognize a child's difficulty as largely biological, they will not blame the child for "laziness" or "touchiness" and will help make the environment less traumatic and frightening for the youngster.

For a long time it was thought that if children were not well behaved or if they had emotional problems it was entirely the parents' fault. In recent years, however, we have come to recognize that such an ascription of "blame" is probably unjust. In fact, some infants often provoke certain negative behaviors on the part of even the most patient and devoted parents. Indeed, it is now recognized that a child can be as much a factor in the emotional disturbance of his parents as the parents can be in the emotional disturbance of the offspring.

This phenomenon is illustrated in the following case. The mother was a warm, affectionate, outgoing woman who loved to touch and fondle her baby. But the infant was cold and unresponsive in temperament and showed displeasure and annoyance when she attempted to cuddle him. Although the mother wanted to nurse the child, he rejected the nipple. After months of trying to be affectionate without effect, the mother gave up and became bitter, passive, and resigned. At a deeper level, she felt that the infant had rejected an essential part of her as a person and this left her feeling chronically hurt and depressed. If one saw this depressed, apathetic mother at the end of the first year, it would be easy to blame the child's unresponsiveness on the mother when, in fact, just the reverse happened to be the case.

The point of the illustration is that it is fruitless to "blame" either parents or children when emotional disturbance appears. In point of fact, it is often difficult to assess what the real origins of the problem are. All that one can do is get the best possible picture of the situation as it exists now and try to help parents with it. In the illustration above, for example, it would be important to help the mother to see that she was not responsible for her infant's reaction to her ministrations. In summary, we recognize today that a child can shape parental behavior as easily as parents shape the behavior of their offspring.

2 Mental Development in the Infant

As adults, we are in the habit of gauging an individual's intellectual ability by his verbal skills. Because the very young child has learned few words during the first two years of life, however, it is easy for us to miss the enormous gains he makes in intellectual powers. While these powers are less differentiated than they will be later, we can still note three major intellectual complexes that develop during the first two years of life. These three complexes are the symbolic function, the world of permanent objects located in space and time, and the system of implicit logical processes.

The Symbolic Function

During the first weeks of life, the child is mindful of sounds. It is not clear whether he distinguishes voice sounds from noise or music. Crying is his main vocalization but he is beginning to make other "mewing" and "throaty" sounds, which will in a few months become phonemes—the basic sounds of his language. In the infant's babbling, he produces all the sounds to be found in any of the world's languages. From these sounds he progressively selects those that are closest to the ones he hears people about him make. Any infant can learn any language, but once he begins to shape his vocalizations in particular directions, the malleability of the vocal apparatus is reduced. The older children get, the more difficult it becomes to learn languages other than their own. After about the age of twelve, learning new languages without an "accent" is very difficult.

Language is, however, more than the production of recognizable sound patterns. Some mynah birds speak very well but they do not possess language. Crucial to human language is the *symbolic function,* the ability to comprehend and utilize socially constructed representations of reality. The symbolic function does not usually begin to appear until the end of the first year of life and does not really come into full play until the end of the second year.

To be sure, the infant can use some forms of representation. Several months after birth the infant will smile at the sound of his mother's voice even before he sees her. He has reacted to a *sign* and taken her voice (a part of the mother) for the whole (the mother herself). Likewise, several months after birth the child may begin to salivate when he hears the kettle sing, because this "singing" always has preceded his being fed. In this case, the "singing' has become a conditioned *signal* of food to come. In his ability to respond to signs and signals, however, the infant does not differ from animals, who can also respond to signs and signals. Most dog owners, for example, have a phrase such as "do you want out" that will bring the dog prancing to his feet and scratching at the door. The dog is responding to a signal, to a different sound, and not to a "meaningful" set of words.

With the emergence of the symbolic function, however, the infant goes far beyond the passive response to signs and signals. With the aid of the symbolic function the child can, for the first time, create and produce his *own* symbols. When a child can produce a symbol at will, to convey a wish or command, he gives evidence of having attained the symbolic function. Between the first and second years, children gain rapidly in the words they can understand and produce, and in the grammatical constructions they can generate.

It is important to emphasize, however, that the symbolic function implies more than the production of language. Many other types of symbolic activity also emerge as a result. Only after about the age of two, for example, do we hear reports of dreams and only then do we begin to observe dramatic play wherein children dress up like daddy or mommy. The creation of original symbols is also a consequence of the general symbolic function whose appearance, more than anything else, allows the child to become a truly social being. ("Look, Mommy, a butterfly," says the child, holding up a potato chip.)

The World of Permanent Objects

Sometimes, when a passenger is sitting in a train at a station and the adjacent train starts to move, he cannot perceive which train is moving and which one is standing still. While this happens on rare occasions to the adult, it is the only kind of experience the young infant knows. This is true because the young infant does not clearly distinguish between experiences that come about as a result of his own actions (such as the disappearance of mother when he turns his head) and those which are brought about by the actions of others (such as the disappearance of mother when she walks out of the room). One aspect of this mode of experience is that the child is not aware that anything exists over and above that which is immediately present to his senses.

Jean Piaget, the Swiss psychologist, has shown that the child overcomes this mode of experience in a discernible sequence of stages that are roughly related to age and the development of perceptual and motor abilities. During the first few months of life the infant merely persists in certain actions like sucking after the bottle is removed or looking at the point where the mother disappeared as if these actions would make the bottle or mother reappear. Between the third and seventh months of life the infant gradually begins to separate the object from his actions upon it. He begins to behave as if he thought objects had movements of their own. At this stage the infant will look at the point where an object hit the ground rather than fixate upon the point where it was released. During this period, too, the infant can look away and then back at the same object, which suggests he is beginning to sense its permanence apart from his own movements.

Between the ages of eight and ten months, the young child begins to look for hidden objects. What he does now — and did not do before — is actively to remove a barrier (say, a blanket or pillow) that is obscuring his view of an object. That is to say, the infant begins to coordinate his actions with the independent movements and position of objects. At this stage, however, the child shows a kind of perseveration and believes the object always remains in the place where he found it. If the child finds his ball behind the chair and sees it roll behind the couch, he crawls over to the chair and looks behind it rather than behind the couch.

During the second year of life, the young child makes good progress in dealing with hidden objects, and, by the end of the second year, he can find an object that has been displaced several times. He can now find a toy that was first placed behind a chair and then put into a closet. This indicates that the two-year-old grasps that the object is not only independent of his own actions but also independent of particular places and other objects. It means, too, that the child has elaborated an elementary conception of space in which he and other objects are located. He can also follow the displacements of objects, which reflects a beginning sense of temporal series of events. Finally, in his efforts to remove barriers from in front of hidden objects, the infant shows an early sense of causal relations.

By the end of the second year, therefore, the elaboration of the object world has gone quite far. Not only does the two-year-old child recognize the independence of objects from himself but he has also begun to locate himself and objects in a spatial, temporal, and causal frame of reference.

The Emergence of Reason

Traditionally, the "age of reason" has always been said to be six or seven. It is certainly true that explicit verbal reasoning emerges at that period. By the end of the second year of life, however, one can already observe an implicit logic and reasoning in the behavior of the young child. While the child is not aware that he is reasoning, it is clearly evident in his behavior.

A number of different investigations have illustrated the implicit reasoning of young children. In one study, a number of interesting lures (candy, little toys) were tied to short strings, which had to be pulled to attain the lures. The problem was complicated because the strings sometimes overlapped in deceptive ways. To attain a particular lure, the young child had to disentangle the correct string. Among six-month-old youngsters, the problems were approached in a trial-and-error way. But among the two-year-olds there was abundant evidence that they understood the relationships involved and they solved the problem by pulling the right string to get the lure.

In another study, young children were shown a jar with a pellet in it, which they were to retrieve. At fifteen months of age, most young children tried to retrieve the pellet by shaking the bottle. When this turned out to be unsuccessful, the children inserted their fingers into the bottle and tried to "hook" the pellet with their fingertips. By age two, however, the children immediately turned the bottle over to retrieve the pellet. Again, this behavior reflects a fairly good understanding of the causal and spatial relationships involved and some implicit reasoning.

Piaget has demonstrated the implicit reasoning of the two-year-old in still another way. He showed a two-year-old a piece of candy in his hand, which he then closed and placed under a hat on the table. While his hand was under the hat, Piaget released the candy but closed his fist again before he withdrew it from beneath the hat. When the child was asked to find the candy, he first opened Piaget's hand and, finding nothing there, proceeded to search beneath the hat, where he found the hidden sweet. The candy then made a more permanent disappearance as the child put it into his mouth.

Notice the implicit reasoning inherent in this sequence of actions. In the first place, the child could not have solved the problem simply by "looking" or "seeing" what Piaget did, since the child never actually saw Piaget put the candy under the hat. To look under the hat for the candy, the child had to reason somewhat as follows: "Candy in the hand, hand under the hat, candy not in the hand, candy under the hat." It is important that we do not dismiss such simple inferential behavior as trivial because it marks an important new milestone in the evolution of the young child's intelligence.

By the age of two, therefore, the child has: 1) attained the symbolic function, including the beginning of language; 2) gone far towards constructing a world of permanent objects and a notion of himself as a discrete entity within that world and 3) demonstrated an implicit logic in his actions—a forerunner of the more explicit reasoning powers that will emerge later in development. In the next few years, the child will progressively coordinate language, objects, and reasoning to arrive at a more integrated system of thinking about himself and the world. While this world view will still be different from that held by adults, it will also be a great advance over the limited world view of the two-year-old.

3 Personal and Social
Development
in the Young Child

Children between the ages of two and five show many new abilities and powers compared to infants and toddlers, but retain some ties with their recent past. Although toilet training is usually complete by age two-and-a-half or three, even four- and five-year-olds occasionally have accidents. Likewise, crying fits and tantrums, characteristic of the infancy period, are not unusual in children of nursery school age. Many young children continue to nap for several hours in the afternoon and many continue to nap even when they are in half-day kindergarten.

If there are continuities between infancy and early childhood, there are some apparent discontinuities as well. Although infants may look at and make overtures to other infants, true social interaction between like-age children does not usually appear until about the age of three or four. Likewise, it is only after the age of two that the symbolic function really comes into its own. Only after the age of two, for example, do children really begin to invent words like the three-year-old who said, "I'm sick, I think I have diaperiah." Early childhood also bears witness to the first reports of dreams and night terrors. It is also the age at which children begin to engage in symbolic play such as putting on mommy's hat, or clomping about in daddy's shoes.

Individual differences that began to appear in infancy become much more pronounced during the preschool years, when young people take on more recognizable personalities. During their early childhood, one gets hints about which children will be aggressive, which will be shy and quiet, which will be happy and outgoing, and which will be secretive and conspiratorial. While there are many transformations in these tendencies, some facets of personality that emerge in early childhood persist throughout life. Such temperamental dispositions are probably a direct product of genetic endowment and social experience, which, once crystallized, appear to be self-reinforcing and self-perpetuating through the whole life cycle.

Growth in early childhood is of many different kinds and includes physical increases in height and weight, changes in body conformation and muscular control, increased self-awareness, greatly enhanced mental and language powers, and broad new areas of social awareness and interaction. The succeeding sections will describe a limited sampling of the new achievements and attainments of the early childhood period.

Physical Development

During the preschool years, physical growth slows down somewhat from the rapid pace of infancy. In contrast to the 7 or 8 inches in height gained by the infant during the first and second years of life, the preschool child gains only 3 to 4 inches a year in stature. Height during the preschool years provides a reasonably good index of final adult stature. At age two-and-one-half, for example, the child has attained about 50 percent of her final stature at adulthood. A girl who is 33 inches at age two-and-one-half would be expected to be 5 feet 6 inches as an adult. In contrast, a child does not attain half her adult weight until about age ten. Generally, girls tend to be somewhat smaller and lighter than boys through early childhood, as they will be in adulthood.

At about age five, the termination of the preschool period, the average boy is about 43 or 44 inches in height and weighs about 43 pounds. Girls are close behind both in height and in weight. By age five, the child's body proportions have changed as well. The preschool child's head is about one-fourth her body size and reflects that the brain has reached 90 percent of its adult weight at age five. At age five, however, the top-heaviness is beginning to give way to the scrawny scarecrow body appearance characteristic of the elementary school years.

While the preschool child is growing in size and weight, she is also becoming more skillful in both large- and small-motor activities. The two-year-old can not only walk but she can also open doors and cupboards, pick things up and drop them. By the age of five, the child has developed some rather fine motor skills and will usually be able to get at least partly dressed by herself (with the exception, perhaps, of not being able to button buttons, zip zippers, or tie her shoes), can pour drinks from a large container, and unwrap candy bars. Large-muscle skills have also developed apace, and many four- and five-year-old children can ride bicycles as well as tricycles. At this age, children also go up and down jungle gyms with ease and considerable enjoyment.

The activity level of young children always amazes adults, who wonder how they keep it up. Within a short period of time, a four-year-old will go up and down a slide, ride a tricycle, get into a fight, grab something to eat, and be off to the jungle gym. In part, this activity level is made possible by the young child's faster metabolism and heart rates, which give proportionately more oxygen to the blood than is true for adults. Hence children tire less easily and recover more quickly. The relatively faster heart rate and metabolism of children also explains why they are less sensitive to extremes of heat and cold than are adults. Preschoolers will play in the snow with glee while adults stand shivering nearby. It is no wonder, then, that preschool children often wear out their parents and teachers.

A negative consequence of the preschool child's high activity level is that she may get into dangerous situations. Running into the street, eating pills from the medicine closet, pushing a wire into a wall socket are some of the dangerous situations young children are prone to. In this connection, I believe that it is well to instill in the child some *healthy fears*. When a child runs into the street it is appropriate for the parent to be upset and to communicate this distress to the child. This can be done through voice tone and expression, "Don't ever do that again." The parent's emotional distress and verbalization will help to build in the child a healthy fear of running in the street that will eventually work automatically. Unfortunately, young children learn only by such emotional displays and are not yet susceptible to learning by a calm discourse about the "dangers" of running into the street.

Sexual Differentiation

"Girls, ugh" is a frequent expression among young elementary school boys who are at great pains to show their distaste for the opposite sex. Although some of these attitudes filter down to young children, they are much less in evidence among preschool youngsters than they will be later. At the preschool level boys and girls play together without constraint and will often model adult behavior. In the preschool, it is not unusual to see a girl bedecked with an apron call a boy dressed in a fire hat, "Come to the table and have your dinner, honey."

It is generally accepted today that many of the behaviors that distinguish boys from girls are learned and do not reflect innate genetic or physiological differences. Traditionally, girls were taught that fighting, climbing, and rough games were not "ladylike." Boys, in contrast, were taught that sewing, cooking, and dancing were things that "girls do." As a consequence of such training, even young children begin to perceive their sex roles and to behave according to adult expectations. It is not clear yet, however, how such things as women's liberation will affect the upcoming generations. What may happen is that parents will be more sensitive to sex typing and stereotyping and that they will be less restrictive about their children's behavior than were parents in past generations. In today's preschool, for example, boys are to be found in the doll corner or preparing "dinner" on the toy stove.

While it is important to be aware of the extent to which sexual differentiation is culturally imposed, it is also important to recognize the very real biological differences between the sexes. Girls are smaller and lighter than boys and they do have proportionately more fat than muscle contrasted to boys. Girls are, moreover, much less vulnerable than boys to all sorts of environmental contingencies. For example, during the Second World War, European girls suffered less from concentration camp experience than did the European boys. Their growth was less stunted as a result of malnutrition, and they recovered more quickly from deprivation. Likewise, boys suffer from *early childhood autism,* a schizophrenia-like disorder in which absence of emotional attachments is a dominant symptom, four times as much as girls. Many more examples could be given of the very real physical and physiological differences between the sexes.

The recognition of established sex differences, however, should not be taken, as it has been in the past, as an excuse for discrimination. What is needed is a greater respect for these differences and an acceptance of the fact that they are just that, differences, which may all have intrinsic value. Nor should the recognition of differences obscure the very real similarities between the sexes. Women, no less than men, need to develop a sense of personal identity that confirms them as individuals apart from their husbands and children. Indeed, it is probably society's lack of recognition of women's need for personal identity, for a sense of individual worth which, more than anything else, has provoked the new feminism. We need to help girls and boys to consider a wide range of occupations and life-styles beyond those conventionally allocated to men and women.

Psychological Development

"Let me do it myself" is in many ways the central theme of early childhood. It is often hard for adults, who have been feeding, dressing, and getting things for themselves for many years, to appreciate a young child's feelings in such matters. The urge to do things by herself reflects the child's new-found motor abilities and, even more, her new-found sense of self and initiative. She is busy discovering that "I am me," and one way to discover "me" is to do things for herself. It is for this reason that parents are well advised not to do for young children what they can do for themselves. Waiting a few moments for a child to button herself up or pull up her own zipper is well worth it in terms of the child's budding sense of being able to get things going on her own.

To be sure, the preschool child, like the elementary school child and the adolescent, experiences that basic conflict that confronts us throughout the whole life cycle — the conflict between the wish to grow up and the wish to remain a child. The preschool child may go back to earlier patterns when a new baby comes into the house, or when she is tired or frustrated. Such backsliding is entirely natural and happens to all young children. If it is accepted as what it is, a momentary hesitation, a pause in the rapid pace of growth, the child will rapidly regain her momentum and initiative. Parents can, however, engender a sense of guilt in the young child if they treat her momentary lapses as malicious actions. While there are many different ways to handle such backsliding, the important thing is to regard it as a normal part of growth and not as a moral lapse.

One of the great charms of the preschool years is the young child's creativity. Again and again, her verbal expressions give voice to fresh new ways of looking at reality. One young man, looking up at some wispy clouds, cried, "Look, Daddy, I can see God's fingers." Another young man, whose lusty baritone had to be stilled so that the other children could keep the melody, lamented, "I used to sing pretty good until they invented tunes." The preschool child is also capable of a rather straightforward reasoning and empathy. Our four-year-old son, Ricky, asked, "Dad, why don't you get rid of this old car?" I said, in return, "Well, I'm pretty old. Would you like to get rid of me, too?" To which he replied, "Well, no, not yet. You still work pretty good!"

One could go on, but the preschool years are, in a very real sense, the "magic years." The young child is so charming in her eagerness for life and her creative approach to it that this period is by far the favorite stage of childhood as far as most adults are concerned. There is another quality of young children that should be mentioned, their lack of vengefulness. Young children fight and then play together again; they do not bear a grudge. It always seemed to me that it was this quality that Jesus had in mind when he said, "Only as ye . . . become like young children shall ye enter the gates of heaven."

Social Development

In the center of a sandbox in a nursery school stood a steam shovel. Two boys were looking at the shovel, when the teacher told them to "share" it and to "take turns." Within moments, the boys were fighting and each one claimed it was his turn. Although "sharing" and "taking turns" are familiar concepts to older children and adults, they are foreign to the young child. Actually, young children often regard toys as an extension of themselves, so that sharing is like giving away part of "me." The violent fights young children get into over possessions reflect the young child's close attachment to things. One of the accomplishments of the preschool period is to shift the child's allegiance from things, such as toys, to young people his own age. This shift from things to age mates is a crucial task of socialization during the early childhood years.

Parents and teachers can help children in such situations by recognizing how important possessions are to children. Offering rewards for sharing, while it is a natural reaction, is not very helpful because it ignores the child's investment in the object. A more successful procedure is to acknowledge ownership or temporary possession. Giving a child a name tag to place on whatever toy she is allowing another child to play with is a big help. The name tag gives public acknowledgment to the child's ownership. Often underlying a child's unwillingness to share is the very public loss of ownership this entails.

Another facet of socialization during this era is the progressive overcoming of *egocentrism*. The young child, because of intellectual limitations, cannot put herself in another child's position and see her point of view; this is egocentrism. It helps account for many aspects of the young child's behavior. It is, in part, because the child cannot take her friend's point of view that she has difficulty in sharing. Likewise, two preschool children at play often talk "at" rather than "to" one another. One says, "My dog is going to the hospital to get fixed," while the other says, "Grandma sent me five dollars for my birthday." True communication involves taking the other person's point of view, and young children cannot really accomplish this, at least not when the other person's point of view is different from their own.

When children deal with adults, another aspect of egocentrism comes into play. A young mother has a headache, and lies down in her room with the shades drawn. Her four-year-old son rushes in and tugs her arm to come and see the fort he has built. She says she has a headache and asks to be left alone, but the child persists until the tone of his mother's voice tells him it would be more prudent to withdraw. It would be wrong to attribute the child's behavior to thoughtlessness and insensitivity rather than to what it is, namely, intellectual immaturity. He was, after all, quite incapable of putting himself in his mother's place and of grasping her need for quiet and rest.

Learning to share and to take turns, to take the other person's point of view, and to listen to the other person while she is talking are part of what the young child has to accomplish before she enters public school. In addition, she must learn to control her feelings and emotions so that she can verbalize her anger and disappointment without acting on them. When a frustrated child says to another, "You give me that doll or I'll—I'll explain it to you," she has made the transition from expressing her feelings through action to expressing them verbally. All of these facets of socialization are required for the child to be incorporated into the peer culture of the elementary school years.

Sociocultural Change

The change in attitude towards the education and rearing of young children over the past decades is a dramatic example of the effect of sociocultural change. Prior to the Sputnik in 1957, early childhood education, as embodied in the nursery school, was regarded as a luxury. Only about a tenth of all three- to five-year-old children attended such schools. Today, however, pre-schools are looked upon as a necessity for capitalizing upon the preschool child's rapidly developing mental abilities. There is, however, considerable controversy about what the best sort of program for young children should be. Indeed, parents have more alternatives at the preschool level than they have at any other point in their child's educational career.

While it is not possible to enumerate all the possible alternatives, some of them can be described. At one end of the spectrum are schools that focus upon the child's achieving certain tool skills by the end of a specified year. The explicit aim of such schools is to prepare children for elementary school. Many franchised schools, and to some extent the Montessori schools, tend to be oriented in this direction. At the other end of the spectrum are the so-called "open," or informal, schools that emphasize the development of such traits as independence and creativity. In fact, the differences are matters of emphasis, and most good preschools both prepare children for school and help them to develop desirable personality traits.

It seems to me that most good preschools, whatever their avowed aims, share many characteristics and practices. In such schools, the programs are always adapted to the rhythm and pace of each child's unique pattern of development. That is why I call such schools "growth preschools." In such schools it is recognized that young children are in a transition between the almost total dependence of babyhood and the relative independence of childhood. Accordingly, the theme of the growth schools' activities (whatever their particular emphasis) is "continuity with the past, preparation for the future." Growth preschools work to help children make the transition from the helplessness of infancy to the relative independence of childhood.

Play is a vital part of the activities in a growth preschool. Children are encouraged to squish about with finger paints and with clay, even to get sopping wet at the sink. For young children this kind of play provides a link with their past, when dabbling in mud and water was a favorite pastime. At the same time, the youngsters are given the chance to play in ways that teach them something about growing up and what their future roles will be. I recall one four-year-old girl playing mother to another little girl who had done something "bad." The first child threatened, "I'm so angry at you, I could spit." By imitating her mother (and a good imitation it was), she was learning to express her feelings rather than acting them out.

The principle of continuity with the past and preparation for the future is reflected in the facilities provided by growth preschools. Equipment for large-muscle activities — jungle gyms, slides, big wooden blocks — hearken back to the child's past when he was acquiring large-muscle skills. At the same time, the growth preschool also prepares the child for the future by having playthings that require fine motor coordination. Beads for stringing, puzzles, button boards, snap blocks, plastic nuts and bolts — all encourage children to learn skills they'll need for tying their shoes, for holding a pencil, and so on. In most cases, children know better than anyone else how much and what kind of muscle practice they need, and good teachers let them follow their own inclinations in such matters.

Growth preschools also provide the comforts and reassurances young children need, while offering them the opportunity to mature socially and emotionally. The preschool teacher must be ready to scoop up the weary youngster who tells him or her, "I need a lap." On the other hand, the teacher must also be ready to let the child go a few minutes later when she decides to leave the lap and join her friends. At times the teacher needs to be authoritative and to require relatively independent behavior from the children. When it comes to putting on coats, for example, the teacher should expect the children to do this for themselves. He or she should usually not do for a child what she is capable of doing for herself.

Good teachers also recognize that preschool children are less able to control their emotions than school-age youngsters. They get angry quickly and are likely to express their anger in physical action. One boy who was upset by the presence of a new baby brother in his house needed only the slightest provocation to bite through the sleeve of his friend's jacket. With most young children, fortunately, anger abates as rapidly as it develops; preschool youngsters rarely engage in vengeful actions. However, the emotional instability of preschool children makes them particularly sensitive to the moods of others, and it takes only one child who is out of sorts to set the whole group on edge. Good teachers in growth schools must possess special skills in dealing with children who sometimes lose control.

In social activities, too, the growth preschool strives for continuity between the children's past and their future. Young children need some time to play by themselves in their own way, and the growth preschool gives youngsters the chance to select the toys they want to play with, whether these be form boards, puzzles, trucks, or dolls. At some time during each day, however, the teacher brings the children together for group activities such as story time, show-and-tell, and snacks.

When there are teacher aides in the preschool, the class can be broken up into smaller groups for projects like learning to play a zither or finding out what kinds of things float and what kinds do not. Children vary tremendously in their readiness for group interaction. The preschool teacher must use all of his or her skill and intuition to guide the shy child into social activities, being careful not to push her faster than she is able to go.

In helping preschool children develop socially, the teacher needs to be aware of young children's self-centeredness—their inability to imagine themselves in someone else's position. This quality may have a certain charm, as when a child says, "My tooth hurts, can't you feel it?" But it is also frequently the cause of disputes and quarrels. Because the preschool child cannot take her friend's point of view, she can't understand the other child's wish to play with the fire engine when she wants it, nor can she really understand the concept of taking turns. I remember vividly a boy of four, who, when told it was not his turn on the slide, replied, "It is so my turn because I want it to be."

The emphasis on play in a good growth preschool doesn't mean that the child's intellectual needs are being neglected. A good growth preschool provides plenty of intellectual stimulation in a great many of its activities. When children make ice cream or peanut butter or soup, for example, they learn many facts and concepts in an enjoyable way. While making soup, they learn the names of the vegetables, how various plants grow, the colors of the ingredients, and the differences between things that are raw and things that are cooked. They also learn something about measuring, counting, and adding. Those who criticize the practical arts, such as cooking, as being intellectually sterile should consider how much and how agreeably children learn through such activities.

In helping children progress to a more mature level of thinking, the good preschool teacher respects and values the special logic of preschool youngsters, which has a charm and directness all its own. For example, when our middle son, Bobby, was four, he told me that he was glad we took the station wagon on a trip to the toy store because "it is longer than our other car and it got us there quicker." And how can an adult fault the reasoning of Brooke, a four-year-old girl I know, who remarked, "When you go by water it is better to go by boat, and when you go by air it is better to go by plane."

Young children frequently express a wonderfully original, sensible, and appealing kind of logic and language. A four-year-old getting ready for his bath exclaims, "Look, I'm barefoot all over." A three-year-old, after being tucked into his bed, warns his father, "Don't put out the light. I can't see how to sleep." Or consider the boy whose mother says, "You mustn't pick fights," and who replies, "Oh, Mommy, what can I do when the fight just crawls out of me?"

It would be very sad—a loss to us and to our children—if preschools tried to discourage this inventive use of language. The growth preschool values and encourages the child's original expressions, but at the same time helps to familiarize her with the accepted "grown up" language and concepts she will be using in elementary school.

In describing the growth preschool I have repeatedly referred to the teacher. This is inevitable because the quality of preschool education, perhaps more than any other, depends upon the skill and knowledge of the teacher.

Good preschool teachers come in all sizes and ages and from many backgrounds. What they have in common is a genuine affection for their children and an intuitive understanding of how preschool youngsters think and feel. The skillful teacher acts more like a stage manager than a director—he or she sets the stage for the action but does not direct it. This doesn't mean that the teacher is passive or doesn't have the group under control. The good teacher sets limits and enforces them with kindness and firmness. He or she knows that the best way to calm angry or excited children is to remain calm herself or himself and express verbally the feelings being experienced by the children. For example, he or she might prevent a fight by explaining, "David, you're angry at Eric because he took your truck, and I know you feel like hitting him with that block, but you can tell him how you feel without hitting him."

Children between the ages of three and five are different in many important ways from school-age youngsters, and they need a different kind of school. They are not yet accustomed to thinking abstractly, their language is highly imaginative, their emotions are unstable, and their physical coordination is still poor. They have to learn physically, socially, and emotionally as well as intellectually, and the stimulation they're provided should nourish all the aspects of their personalities. Such overall nourishment for general personality growth is what any good preschool, regardless of whether its emphasis is academic achievement or self-realization, must provide.

Choosing a Preschool for Your Child

Preschools come in many varieties. Private cooperative nursery schools, in which parents participate and contribute to pay the salary of a master teacher, are usually located in churches or other buildings where there is available space. Private nursery schools are run by individuals for profit, and usually have their own building, or buildings, fully paid staff, and full-day as well as part-day programs. Private nursery schools vary widely in orientation and reflect everything from the open orientation of the English infant schools to the more structured programs of the Montessori variety. In recent years, a large number of franchised preschools have come into operation under the auspices of large corporations. Many of these schools emphasize the learning of academic tool skills (reading, writing, arithmetic).

Which school you choose for your child will depend upon your economic resources, the availability of particular schools in your area, your own orientation, and the characteristics of your child. As in the case of the day-care center, the most important consideration is that the teachers are qualified and not overworked by a high child-to-teacher ratio.

Given a good physical plant and qualified teachers, parents need to look at what they can afford and what is convenient.

Last, but not least, is the child. A child who is rather impulsive, unsystematic, and disorganized might profit from a Montessori-type program, while a self-disciplined, creative child might flourish in an open classroom setting. However, since good preschool teachers, in any setting, will adapt to a child's needs, the crucial factor is still to find a good physical plant with a well-trained, competent faculty. Once that is done, preparing the child for preschool follows the same formula described earlier in preparing a child for entrance into a day-care center.

Several Characteristics of Early Childhood

"Daddy, how come you have those lines around your eyes? I don't like them. They are scary." Young children are, if anything, frank and outspoken, but sensitive realists. They usually call the shots as they see them and will say that somebody is ugly or smells bad if that is what they perceive. Young children are also not fooled by adult facades. They see through the syrupy sweet gushing of the woman who really hates children, but they can sense the positive feeling of a quiet, retiring man who has a genuine affection for little people. Young children have no mystical abilities in the regard; probably they just respond to cues which we adults tend to ignore.

It is the young child's sensitivity to adult moods and feelings that makes her both a very vulnerable and a very difficult opponent. Because she is sensitive, she can experience rejection and dislike even when the adult tries to cover these up. At the same time, she can also discern when the adult is really serious about a command and when the grown-up can be pushed just a hair's breadth further. Of course, sometimes young children get too sure of themselves and push the adult too far, but for the most part young children gauge adult intentions with considerable skill.

If the young child is at times a realist, she is also a visionary. The two traits are really not that discrepant and often go together in adults. The individual who seeks reality in all its harshness and bleakness must, out of necessity, envision a better world. Great statesmen, like great religious leaders, share the young child's unblinking appreciation of reality, but also her capacity for envisioning a better world. But there is a difference. The adult envisions a better world on the order of the present one, whereas the better world of the child is the fairy-tale world of candy castles and lollipop trees.

Consequently, a young child believes in Santa Claus and in the good fairy who will bring her a quarter if she puts her tooth under a pillow. Young children believe in fairy godmothers, in magic wands and in never-never lands. The possibilities of an old woman who lives in a shoe, a gingerbread man who runs, and a candy house in the forest are not outside the range of possibility. For the young child, these fantasies are every bit as real as his daddy's rough beard and mommy's soft voice.

The World of Self, Home, and Community

"I" and "me" are frequently used terms in the young child's vocabulary. Early in the history of child psychology, investigators spoke of this period as one of "trotzalter" literally: "the age of defiance." This defiance often involves the young child's resisting adult authority and insisting on having her own way. But young children also show pride in their ability to make and do. They come home from nursery school eager to show their artwork and hear it praised by adults. They tug adults into playrooms to show them block towers, garages, and well-set tea tables. So however strong-willed the young child is, her emerging sense of self is still vulnerable and she needs the support of adult praise and encouragement.

All this is to say that the young child needs recognition. At this stage, particularly ages three and four, the self is very much a "symbolic" self that is closely tied to the child's name and to other key words such as "I" and "me" and "mine." This is why it is so important to know young people's names and to get them right. Recognition of a child's name, of her creations, and of her activities, gives reality to the symbols by which the child identifies and knows herself. Answering a child's questions is another way of recognizing and rewarding her symbolic expression of herself. The attachment of children to things also reflects the young child's budding sense of self, which, at this stage, she experiences through symbols and symbolic activities of her own construction.

A concrete example of the importance the young child places upon names can be observed in the preschool. When two children in the group share the same name (say, Nancy), they will inevitably call one another by their full names: "Nancy Jones" or "Nancy Green." They do this to insure that no one will confuse the two Nancys with one another. Likewise, when a young man named Robert, but called "Bobby," is called Robert, he will reply, "No, not Robert, Bobby," Names are important to all of us, but particularly to children, who regard their names as a critical part of their identities.

Within the home the young child is a constant source of amusement, exasperation, and amazement. She is amusing in her body size and proportions, and in the contrast between these and her adult-like verbal pronouncements. At the same time, she is exasperating in her demands for time and attention, for food, for help with her clothes and with the television set. Sometimes she amazes parents with her feats of memory, of motor skill, and of psychological acumen. It always comes as a surprise, for example, when a four-year-old says, "Hello, Harry," to a man she saw only once a year earlier. More than anything else, of course, young children are a source of personal gratification because they are verbally and physically open in their expression of love and affection towards parents.

As far as the community is concerned, it was, until recently, little concerned with preschool-age children. This is changing, however, with the advent of programs such as Head Start, television productions such as "Sesame Street" and "Mr. Rogers' Neighborhood," and as the day-care concept comes into more general prominence. Head Start and day-care centers are, in effect, community centers that must be inspected and licensed, and whose teachers must be accredited. Inspection and accreditation are state functions that will be increasingly brought into play as such facilities become common. The community looks after young children by insuring that the facilities that serve young people meet minimum professional and safety standards.

Giants frequently appear in fairy tales for children, and one encounters them in stories such as "Jack and the Beanstalk" and "The Brave Little Tailor." To the young child who stands barely three feet tall, adults do appear to be giants. They are giants, moreover, who can give out punishment, who can roar with outrage, and who can, at times, be childish in their pettiness. Not only does the young child's world abound in giants, it also abounds in giant-size chairs, tables, dishes, doors, and drinking fountains. For the young child, the world is an outsize place for which she is too small.

In general, young children tend to see adults, as well as children, as good or bad, clever or stupid, kind or mean. Again, the characters in fairy tales reflect this mode of thinking and are also drawn in one-dimensional terms. What this means, in regard to child-adult relations, is that when a young child relates to an adult she does so in an all-or-none fashion. If she regards the adult as "good" she will, even if the adult is a stranger, allow herself to be picked up, held, and nuzzled. On the other hand, if the child regards the adult as "bad" she may shrink away in terror to the dismay of the "offending" but well-meaning grown-up.

The young child's tendency to see her parents as "all good" has some interesting consequences. The child often attributes the "bad" qualities, motives, and actions she perceives in parents to other people and to animals. Many of the fears that young children display with regard to "monsters," "wolves," and "tigers" reflect this tendency to attribute "bad" parental qualities to other creatures. This type of attribution or "projection" allows children to persist in the belief that their parents are all good.

Young children also believe that parents are all-powerful and all-knowing. It seems to them that everything in the world is made by or for man to suit his convenience. Parents can, therefore, do anything. Likewise, because parents have answers to all the child's questions and can operate so many different tools, machines, and gadgets, they must be all-knowing as well. In brief, to the young child the parents take on the godlike qualities of omnipotence and omniscience, while negative parental qualities are projected onto other people and animals. This orientation of the child often makes for harmonious relations with his or her mother and father.

Adults in Relation to Young Children

Most adults—whether or not they are parents—like young children. This is true not just because young children are charming and amusing, but also because of their mode of thinking. The young child, who believes in the omniscience of the adult, flatters the adult ego. The small size of the young child brings out protective feelings in the grown-up. In addition, the young child does not threaten the adult either physically or intellectually because there is virtually no contest on either score. The adult can afford to be generous and giving with the young child because she does not threaten any part of the adult ego. This may seem a harsh judgment, but if we are honest, we have to admit that our relations with older children, particularly with adolescents, reflect, in part at least, the extent to which these young people threaten our self of self-esteem and competency.

Obviously, the unthreatening quality of the young child is only one of the many attributes that make her charming to adults. Her openness and creativity, her love of life, and her abundant energy are a joy to see and are rewarding in themselves. But a deeper understanding of the adult's liking for young children must also take into consideration the fact that neither in thought nor action does the young child pose any kind of challenge to the adult ego. On the contrary, she seems to bolster it on almost every count.

4 Mental Development in the Young Child

In young children as in infants, mental abilities are much less separate from one another and from emotions than they will be in later childhood. A school-age child who is unhappy will still be able to function and participate in learning activities. The young child, however, is so beset by distress that it dominates her intellectual as well as her emotional orientation.

The Development of Mental Abilities

Physiognomic Perception

"What an angry painter," someone says while looking at the harsh black and red strokes on a modern painting. This is an example of physiognomic perception—the reading of human motives and emotions into symbolic and expressive materials. Young children use physiognomic perception to a much greater extent than adults do. Such perception may play a part in young children's astute reading of adult personality. By attending to the adult's expressive behavior, young children may gain instant insight into an adult's true feelings.

Physiognomic perception also helps account for the young child's fearfulness in strange situations. The waving of a branch or the flitting of a shadow can take on a frightening quality if it is perceived as reflecting angry forces. The frequent but transient phobias of young children are, in part, attributable to such physiognomic perception. A two-year-old of my acquaintance, for example, became frightened whenever he saw a broken object. This was a display of physiognomic perception. The broken object seemed to the child to betoken a dis-embodied anger that could be unleashed against himself. Physiognomic perception then, reflects the young child's tendency to project onto inanimate objects the angry impulses he or she senses in him or herself and in her or his parents.

Phenomenalistic Causality

Young children show a strong tendency to regard events that happen together as having caused one another. A child who becomes intensely attached to a furry teddy bear or to a blanket demonstrates this sort of causal thinking. Initially, the teddy bear or the blanket was associated with the cessation of feelings of fear or fright, but the child thinks of the bear or blanket as having "caused" her relief. From then on, the child regards the teddy bear or blanket as a protector who will ward off future dangers. The distress young children undergo when separated from a beloved teddy bear attests to the strength of this phenomenalistic thinking and shows, as in the case of physiognomic perception, how closely tied are the feeling and thinking of young children.

As in the case of physiognomic perception, phenomenalistic causality does not entirely disappear as the child grows older; it accounts for the superstition one observes in older children and adults. Many college students, for example, have particular rituals related to exam taking. One young man once took a bath the night before an exam on which he expected to do poorly. In fact, he got a high B. Thereafter, he always took a bath the night before an examination. Unfortunately, the procedure did more for his hygiene than it did for his grade point average. Other young people try a kind of negative thinking ("Oh, I'll never get an A"), as if the entertainment of the idea that they might get A's would prevent this from occurring.

Phenomenalistic causality can also explain why young children can believe in the magic happenings of fairy tales. In a world where phenomenalistic causality reigns, anything can happen and can cause anything else. In such a world it is entirely possible that making a wish could bring about its fulfillment or that waving a wand could produce a coach and horses. Thus, when young children discover that if they pull up the shade they can see the sun, some will henceforth believe that raising the shade brings out the sun. Young children's beliefs in magic thus reflect their immersion in phenomenalistic causality.

Norminal Realism

Language development is very rapid in early childhood, but the child's understanding of the arbitrariness of language lags far behind her grasp of linguistic forms. The average four-year-old thinks that the name of the sun resides within the sun and is as intrinsic to it as its heat or light. If you ask a young child whether it is possible to call the television set another name, such as Spodnunk, she denies that this is possible because she believes that every object has only one name, that is has always possessed that name, and will never be able to change it.

Parents often unconsciously perpetuate this word magic by their prohibitions about saying certain words. When a young child is told not to say a particular word, she interprets this as meaning the saying of the word will bring some dreaded event. Many children tempt fate by saying forbidden words in the privacy of their rooms while they wait, in fear and trembling, for the inevitable clap of thunder and the lightning. One reason young children get so upset by being called names by other children is their underlying belief that being called a name, say, "stupid," may actually have the effect of making them stupid. Here again is a melding of cognitive and feeling functions in the thought of the young child.

Rote Learning

It has often been said that the young child is an eager and facile learner. This is true enough, but look at what young children learn with such eagerness and alacrity. Read a story to a young child several times and she will know it by heart. Indeed, she gets annoyed if the adult, through carelessness, departs from the standard version. This is good rote learning. Another kind of learning in young children is reflected by the youngster who can, from a stack of records, choose the one she wants played without being able to read the label. This is an example of astute discrimination learning.

Rote and discrimination learning, however, about exhaust the young child's learning repertoire. The child's use of these learning modes is, moreover, highly selective and arbitrary. Young children have a tendency not to learn people's names, although such learning should be easy for them. Because of their own egocentrism, however, they really take little interest in other people's names and don't take the trouble to learn them. Also, if parents decide to teach a child her letters and her numbers and she does not want to learn, she will not, although she is quite capable of doing so. In a very real sense the young child is an extraordinarily selective and arbitrary learner.

The learning of young children is limited in still another direction. Parents are often annoyed because young children have so much difficulty learning to say "thank you" and "please." Many parents complain, "No matter how many times I tell her, she always forgets." Such "forgetting" is, however, more a matter of intellectual immaturity than it is of stubborn boorishness. Saying "thank you" and "please" presupposes the acquisition and comprehension of the general rules—"when you ask for something, say please" and "when you are given something, say thank you"—and their application in new and varied situations. But young children are simply not capable of this level of abstraction and cannot learn general rules of this sort.

Nowhere is the young child's difficulty with rules more evident than in her attempts to play games such as ticktacktoe, checkers, and Monopoly. To play any one of these games the child must incorporate and abide by a certain fixed number of rules, but most young children cannot do so—to the lasting frustration of their older siblings who soon tire of trying to teach them and who often complain to the parents that the little ones "cheat." By the age of six or seven, however, the attainment of new mental abilities makes rule learning, and hence game playing, possible.

The young child has a long way to go before her or his thinking will be as objective and relatively free from emotional determination as it is in the older child and the adult. The young child really operates as a whole, and her or his thinking and feeling are never divorced from one another. In a very real sense, and more than at any other later age, the young child is very much an emotional, motivational, and intellectual totality.

5 Age Profiles

Some people, including some professional child-watchers, react negatively to the description of particular age groups such as the two-year-old or the four-year-old. Their argument is that individual differences are so great and growth patterns so diverse that any delineation of common characteristics for a particular age level is bound to be deceptive and misleading. One can, however, agree with the fact of wide individual differences in behavior without denying characteristics common to a particular age. Children are, after all, growing organisms whose development shows an organization, pattern, and direction that is characteristic of the species.

It would be strange indeed if there were not normative patterns of growth and maturation within a species. To be sure, the use of an arbitrary time unit, such as a year, to categorize certain behaviors has dangers in that more significant changes might be observed if we use two-year or half-year intervals. The use of the year as a unit for categorizing behavior can, however, be justified because it is convenient—it is the unit used in school grouping and hence a label we attach to children—and because it does in fact show up interesting differences.

Accordingly, the descriptions of the unique features of children at different age levels must be taken as an abstraction, an ideal if you will, to which no child will conform in every detail but to which most children will conform to a certain extent. Such an approach has advantages that seem to outweigh the danger to taking the norms too literally. One advantage is that in working with children we are able to have a rough gauge as to whether the behaviors we observe are age-appropriate rather than, say, defects of character. If we know that most six-year-olds "take" things from schools and doctors' offices we can see the behavior in perspective and deal with it more objectively and reasonably. Likewise, if we know that most six-year-old children no longer wet the bed, we may be moved to action if we know a six-year-old who still wets. It is with these considerations in mind that the following age descriptions are offered. If the reader will remember that these are norms only and that deviations are not necessarily bad or abnormal, the descriptions can be useful orientations for living and working with children at particular age levels.

The One-Year-Old

Chronological age is a convenient reference point, but it by no means always, if ever, signals the completion of particular behaviors and the onset of new ones. At one year of age, the infant is very much in transition and there is nothing new and entirely complete to mark her first birthday. Many of the motor, social, and intellectual skills that she will master later have been only partly attained at this way station.

Motorically, the one-year-old is just beginning to show promise of things to come: she is just beginning to pull herself up to an erect position and to pull herself along. In a few more months she will be able to become erect alone and to walk without support. In the same way, she just begins to give evidence, in grasping for a spoon, in pushing blocks, and in holding crayons, of the more elaborate use of these objects she will display in a few more months.

In other domains the infant shows other preliminary skills. She is just developing the ability to "let go," and delights in dropping things outside her playpen or crib and in seeing her parents fetch them back. She is beginning to grasp the orientation of herself and things in space, and can turn a bottle so that she can insert her fingers to attain a desired object. In placing objects in a pattern, she sometimes puts them into a line and so demonstrates a beginning grasp of the notion of seriation.

Language growth is also very much in transition at one year of age. The infant listens intently to adult language and repeats words she likes, finds interesting, and can echo with her powers of imitation. Her passive receptive vocabulary is already large and she can respond to commands such as "Give it to me." She tries to use language socially to attract attention and sometimes, or so it seems, to evoke smiles in admiring adults. Much of her language is still "expressive jargon," incomprehensible speech production that serves as a kind of vocal accompaniment to her actions.

In the social domain, the one-year-old is very conscious of adult presence and she will repeat actions that won her adult laughter. She shows a wide range of emotions, including fear, rage, love, anger, and jealousy. Many children at this age show a fear of strangers and cry when their parents leave them alone or in the room with unfamiliar adults.

In other ways, however, the one-year-old shows new signs of beginning independence. She wants to feed herself—with her fingers, of course—and is annoyed when someone helps her when she has chosen to do it herself. But she is also more cooperative when being changed and dressed than she was before. She seems more sensitive to moods and to the feelings of those about her, and shows a greater readiness to modulate her own reactions in accord with these perceptions. Her social skills are still in the bud stage, but there are signs that the bud will soon open to full flower.

The Eighteen-Month-Old

Growth is very rapid during the first months and years of life. In six months, the eighteen-month-old has gained several inches in height and is now 30 to 33 inches tall. She has made similar gains in weight and weighs a good 20 to 27 pounds—about triple her birth weight. In six months she has added a comparable number of teeth and now sports a respectable dozen, to bite as well as to chew with. While she still sleeps a good thirteen hours or so, she now takes only one nap during the day.

Motor control has increased apace. At eighteen months, the average toddler puffs along at a rapid, flat-footed pace, reminiscent of the movements of long-distance walkers. Other motor skills attest to her new-found coordination. She can aim her backside at a chair and get it there with reasonable accuracy. Stairs are a real challenge, and she loves to bump down them without help and to crawl up them without assistance. The problem at this age is often to keep the toddler away from the stairs.

Small-motor control is also better than it was at age one, but her performance is not consistent. With some effort, she can get one block to sit upon another, but is likely to knock them over if she tries to build a tower of three. At eighteen months, the toddler can pick up a piece of paper, and turn the pages of a book with a sweeping motion that is likely to turn a bunch at a time. Well-coordinated fine motor control is still to be attained.

At eighteen months, the young child's perceptions are considerably sharper than they were even several months before. Her sense of spatial perceptions is such that she knows where things are and can retrieve toys and books from their regular places. More generally, the eighteen-month-old gives evidences of perceiving sequences, of being aware that action patterns have a definite beginning and end. When eating, she puts down her spoon as if to say "That's enough." She begins to use "bye bye" as a sign-off expression to terminated actions, and "all gone" becomes another favorite sign-off phrase. The world is now filled with minor episodes and is no longer an unending stream of events that unceasingly blend into one another.

The eighteen-month-old has also begun to use language to express her wants and desires. Language and action are still far from being fully separated, however, and every "no" is accompanied by vigorous head shaking. Likewise, "eat" is usually said to the tune of some pounding or banging. Passive vocabulary also increases at a rapid pace, and the eighteen-month-old can understand more complex commands, such as "Put the ball on the chair," than she could a year earlier. It is probably true, however, that the child uses many contextual as well as language cues to decipher adult commands.

In other domains, the eighteen-month-old's self-concept is more elaborate than it was a scant six months before. At eighteen months, the child distinguishes between "you" and "me" and makes claims about things being "mine." Emotionally the eighteen-month-old is still quite unstable and is likely to show distress and unhappiness by tantrum-like behavior—lying down, kicking, flailing the air. But she is also making progress towards better self-control by imitating adult behaviors. However, the young child is indiscriminate and will mimic behaviors, such as smoking, that are not as effective as frowns and expressions.

What is important is that she has discovered a useful technique of social learning that will stand her in good stead as she faces the pressures of socialization imposed upon all young children.

The Two-Year-Old

At age two, the average child stands between 32 and 35 inches tall and weighs anywhere from 23 to 30 pounds. He still sleeps more than twelve hours and he requires a nap of one or two hours during the afternoon. When he is awake, however, the two-year-old is going all the time. He has much more motor control than he had a scant six months before, and anything that can be climbed upon or jumped from looks like an inviting and an exciting challenge. Indeed the two-year-old often makes adults nervous when he suddenly appears at the top of the stairs and starts coming down "lickety-split." Language growth is also very rapid during the third year and vies with motoric exuberance as the major theme of this age period.

In the motor domain, the two-year-old is expansive and expressive. Now that he can walk and climb without assistance, he takes great pleasure in his mastery and he uses his control to express his emotions. The two-year-old jumps up and down, laughs and chortles when he is happy; and jumps up and down, cries, and yells when he is unhappy. Small-muscle control is also more in evidence than it was at eighteen months. He can do such things as hold a glass of juice with one hand (a feat that parents often watch with fearful anticipation that the juice will spill). The two-year-old can do other small-motor feats such as stacking a number of blocks and stringing wooden beads. Effective art work such as drawing and painting does not, however become really possible for another year.

Motor, intellectual, and language activity are all of a piece in the two-year-old and he likes to hold and examine things that he is learning to label. In contrast to the eighteen-month-old, the two-year-old looks for hidden toys and shows that he has begun internally to represent external objects and to let the internal representations guide his behavior. This new capacity for internal representation is seen also in the two-year-old's ability to recall events of earlier in the day and to anticipate events later in the day. In a very real sense the time-space world of the two-year-old has begun to expand beyond the immediate here and now to events that are occurring at a somewhat greater temporal and spatial distance.

Goal-seeking behavior at age two reflects this new expansion of the space-time dimension. If a two-year-old sees a ball roll behind one chair and then behind another, he goes immediately to the second chair. At an earlier age he would have gone to the first chair and, not finding the ball, have given up. At two, the child even shows a kind of deductive reasoning. If the adult hides some candy, in a box in a cupboard, the two-year-old can find it. He will move a stool or chair to reach the cupboard. Once there, he will search the various containers until he finds the candy. He is able to reason that if the candy is not in one container, it will be in the next. This reasoning is elementary, but, nonetheless, the child has shown his ability to reason.

Memory is another facet of intellectual ability that shows rather remarkable gains during this period. Not only is the child learning the names of many objects, he retains them and uses them correctly. He also recalls where he left toys and where edible treats are likely to be hidden. This kind of ability is also shown in the two-year-old's capacity for deferred imitation—his ability to see an event at one point in time (say a child pushing a baby carriage) and to imitate that behavior at a later point in time. Memory processes thus reflect and help extend the widened temporal and spatial boundaries of the child at age two.

It is language, however, that is the leading edge of the expansion of the two-year-old's intellectual world. By the age of two most children know about three hundred words and may know as many as a thousand. The child is learning words and grammatical forms at an enormous rate and has already acquired the basic pronouns for talking about himself: "I," "me," "mine." He also produces two- and three-word utterances that reflect a beginning grammatical understanding. Combinations such as "Peter fall down" or "Sally eat candy" are quite common.

For young children particularly, words lack the specificity of meaning and separateness they have for adults. "Peter up" may mean "Pick me up," or "Peter wants to pick it up," or "Peter is up on the chair," and so on. In children at this age, language is very much tied up with action so that the child's actions are often the only clue to the meaning of his language. At this age, too, children very much enjoy the rhythm pattern and musical qualities of language as much as its meaning. One reason children clamor to hear the same story again and again—to the adult's dismay—is that they enjoy the music of the story being read as much as or more than its content.

Within the social sphere, the two-year-old shows mounting evidence of independence from adult assistance and increased interest in children his own age. The two-year-old will often object to mother's directions and will demand to do things for himself, like putting his arms in his jacket and using his spoon. With other children the two-year-old is still quite self-centered, but at least he will sit with other children and play beside them for a while, as if enjoying the companionship of like-sized creatures. When he plays alone, the two-year-old is apt to elaborate upon the mother-baby relationship, perhaps to "work through" his mixed feelings about growing up and becoming more independent.

The two-year-old shows his budding socialization in other ways. When he does something wrong, he tends to look sheepish as if he were beginning to experience guilt about misbehavior. His many negativisms reflect the fact that he is learning to distinguish more clearly between himself and others. Such negativisms have to be understood as part of a normal process of distinguishing between oneself and others. By saying "no" the child asserts his "I" and establishes his sense of individuality. What appears as willfulness in the two-year-old is, fact, the growing self in the process of realization.

The Three-Year-Old

The transition between two and three, as between all age epochs, is gradual rather than abrupt. Three is more motorically adept, more verbal, and more social than two. And yet, although the differences in each domain are only quantitative, when they are all put together the three-year-old seems almost qualitatively different than she was a few scant months earlier.

In the motor realm, the three-year-old still enjoys motor play as she did at two. She now persists for longer periods in such play and she prefers much more complex tasks. When she succeeds in getting a ball out of a puzzle box, she may drop it in again to solve the problem anew. The two-year-old, in contrast, would play with the ball. While the three-year-old can still not draw stick figures, the lines she draws have definite direction and are less repetitive than they were at two.

Large-motor development is also more advanced. At three, the child can ride a tricycle and push a wagon. When she runs, her stopping and starting are more modulated so that she is less likely to bump into people and things at the end of her trajectory. In jumping and climbing she shows similar control. Parents don't wince when they see a three-year-old climb a small ladder to a slide, whereas a two-year-old climbing puts all the adult watchers on edge.

Perceptual motor skills are more advanced than at age two, as well. In her block play, her drawings, and her imitations the three-year-old shows more order and direction than she did a year before. In the process of differentiating between herself and the outside world, she gains a better perception of both, and this is shown in the enhanced organization of her perceptual motor behavior.

Gesell wrote that there is "jargon at eighteen months, words at two years, sentences at three years." As Gesell was quick to point out, however, this guideline is a vast oversimplification of what is actually accomplished at age three. The elaboration of language during this year is quite phenomenal and the grammatical constructions of this period are often astounding to adults ("Don't you do that anymore!"). If one argues that this is mere imitation, one must remember that to imitate such phrases the child must have the ability to reproduce them, and this is just what develops during the third year.

At three, however, language is much less circumscribed than it will be later. Young children talk to themselves while they are playing, eating, or engaging in activities with other children. Language during this period is roughly comparable to an adult's singing or whistling while at work. Such activities are accompaniments to ongoing actions. But the three-year-old's language play is for much more than amusement; it is also for practice. In her constant vocalizing the child is practicing pronounciation, grammatical structure, and inflection. Indeed, three-year-olds, who verbalize constantly, cause many parents (who could not wait for them to speak) to wish that they would shut up.

In the process of this active vocalizing, the three-year-old is also beginning to coordinate words and actions. Words are slowly gaining some executive control over behavior and now an adult verbal command can interrupt the child's actions. Not only words from without, but words from within are beginning to regulate action. At three, the child can deal with a toy hidden under a cover by recalling what the color of the cover was. At this stage, language is just beginning to serve as a mediator between the environment and action, and as one means by which the child can interpose a delay between what she sees and what she reaches out for.

By the time a child is three she no longer needs to assert her individuality as she did at two. She accepts her individuality as she does that of others. Now she wants to be accepted and liked by other people and tries her hardest to please. In part, this may reflect her delight in understanding verbal commands and the pleasure she derives from matching words to actions. At any rate, the three-year-old takes great pride in doing little errands or in fetching her parents' slippers or sweaters.

The three-year-old's social orientation is shown in other ways. She laughs when adults laugh, as if she understood what the joke was all about, and she tries to make adults laugh by laughing herself. The three-year-old is more reticent with other children than she is with adults. In the nursery school, for example, it takes several months before the three-year-olds really begin to play together and to be a genuine group who know one another's names and who engage in joint activities.

To be sure, the three-year-old is not all obedience and deference. She sometimes throws tantrums and may get angry and destroy toys or puzzles she cannot manage. At this age she may experience night terrors and animal phobias. On occasion she also exhibits jealousy and willfulness that are reminiscent of the two-year-old. At the same time, however, she begins to use language as well as action to express her displeasure. And, in general, the three-year-old is beginning to coordinate thought, language, and emotion so that she appears much more stable socially and emotionally than she did at two. But her world is still largely limited to the immediate here and now and to the immediate persons about her. Her adaptations are adequate to this encapsulated world but she has much to learn about the larger world of school and community.

The Four-Year-Old

The four-year-old has consolidated many of the social, emotional, and linguistic gains that were made during the previous year. He appears more at ease in social situations and his language use is quite sophisticated. Indeed, one danger with four-year-olds is mistaking their linguistic processes for their intellectual understanding. Four-year-old children can use words and verbal constructions that are far beyond their level of intellectual comprehension. As a consequence, adults often talk at too abstract a level for the four-year-old level of understanding. But the four-year-old manages to cope with adults and with his peers.

On the motor plane, the four-year-old shows a new confidence in his motor abilities and a new willingness to try new tricks and stunts. He will jump off a low embankment or a couch and will try climbing up a slide the wrong way. His new willingness to try new and exciting motor feats reflects new motor differentiation and coordination of leg and arm muscles. It also reflects the four-year-old's budding sense of initiative, his readiness to do things, and his interest in gaining competence. The four-year-old has learned the joy of success and mastery, and is eager for new experiences of this kind.

In his drawings, the four-year-old reflects both his new perceptual motor skills and his intellectual limitations. When he draws a man, it usually consists of a head, arms, legs, and eyes—with the torso omitted. The child at this stage draws what he knows or thinks is important rather than what he sees. In other perceptual motor behavior the four-year-old can copy single features of an arrangement of objects, but he cannot coordinate them. To illustrate, when he tries to copy an evenly spaced row of six pennies, he does one of two things: either he matches the spacing of the pennies but neglects length (and gets the row too long), or he matches the length but neglects spacing (and makes the row too crowded). Likewise, when a four-year-old is asked whether two pictures of houses are alike or different, he makes his judgment by comparing only the windows or the doors, and may come to different conclusions depending upon which feature of the houses he chooses to compare.

Age four is, more than anything else, the question-asking age, and "why" questions often predominate. It is important to remember that the young child's questions do not reflect the same intent as questions asked at a later age. Many of the young child's questions are aimed at getting and holding the adult's attention. Often, too, the child asks questions in a rhetorical way, in hopes that the adult will ask for his opinion. In this instance he is only too ready to venture a response no matter what the question. In particular, the child's "why" questions reflect his belief that everything in the world has a purpose, a reason for being there. When he asks why the grass is green, he expects an answer like one he himself might venture. If allowed to answer his own question, the child might reply, "To hide the green caterpillars so they won't get eaten by the birds." If the adult answers the question with an explanation involving chlorophyll and the refraction of light, he has missed the intent of the question, and provided an answer too difficult for the child to comprehend. Adults need not worry about giving simple, purposive answers to children's questions. Children will learn the right answers eventually. It is more important that they feel the adult understands their questions.

Perhaps because of his beliefs that everything has a purpose, the four-year-old is quite verbose. When replying to a question he often goes on and on as if each thought that came to his mind was a cause of the next. Likewise, his commentaries on the passing scene tend to be rather prolix. Here is an example quoted from Gesell: "I don't even know that. You almost hit him. Now I will make something else. I can make something different. They are like one another but the other is bigger. That one too." Again, these examples illustrate how elaborate language has become in the short space of two years.

At four, the child shows considerable consolidation of his social gains. Internal control over his own behavior is relatively advanced and he shows a good balance between independence and sociability. He is more self-reliant than ever before and can dress himself (with the exception of tying shoes), and feed himself (with the exception of cutting meat), and go to the toilet by himself. At the same time, the four-year-old enjoys playing with other children just as much as or more than he likes playing by himself. Four-year-old boys and girls have no hesitation in playing with one another, so long as the influence of older male siblings is not there to disrupt the pattern.

While the four-year-old shows much more independence than he did at three he also shows what appear to be unreasonable fears. These may be fears of the dark, of dogs, of birds, and so on. Such fears are not rational, and reasoning with the child about them has little value. A more effective strategy is to accept the child's fear as a reality to him and assure him that someone will be there to help him should he need help.

The four-year-old not only has fears, he also makes up stories, rationalizes and alibis his accidents, and plays the social clown. All of these behaviors bespeak his growing awareness of the social world about him, and of the importance of adult approval for his emerging sense of self-respect and self-esteem. But the vastness and the complexities of the social world into which he is moving are not always easy to deal with. Some of the four-year-old's gaucheries have to be forgiven in the light of his social immaturity and the intricacies of the milieu into which he is trying to integrate himself.

The Five-Year-Old

The five-year-old shows in many ways the completion of the early childhood period. Small- and large-muscle control and co-ordination are quite advanced, and independence training, clothing, eating, and toileting are about complete. Socialization is well advanced and the five-year-old enjoys companions of her own age and may have one or more close friends. Although she is still not ready for formal education she is ready to begin preparing for that type of instruction, for being away from home for full days, and for controlling herself in the absence of parental guidance. With her new motor coordination the five-year-old can do such things as ride a two-wheeler and learn dance steps. In her movements, actions, and posturing, the five-year-old shows a new grace and coordination that is a pleasure to watch. Her small-motor control is a little less advanced but she can use tools from toothbrush to hammer by herself, though without great effectiveness. She can now handle regular puzzles and spinner games and can even throw dice without getting them off the board. Her small-motor behavior thus prepares her for playing table games as well as for writing.

In her intellectual development, the five-year-old is in a kind of transition stage. In making a one-to-one correspondence (matching a pattern of six pennies in a row with a comparable pattern of his own construction) she succeeds by trial and error in coordinating the length of the row and the interval size. When, however, one of the rows is spread out farther than the other, she believes that it contains more pennies than the shorter row. The higher-order coordination of row length and interval size, which involves recognition that what a row gains in length it must lose in density, does not usually appear until the age of six or seven.

In other domains, the five-year-old also shows that she is moving toward the self-direction and control required of the school-age child. She persists longer at tasks and works until she completes a project. She has a more differentiated notion of time and space than she did at four, and can talk meaningfully about tomorrow and yesterday as well as about distant places such as a farm or fire station. And in many ways, the five-year-old seems more painstaking than she was at four. She is more careful, more persevering, and more accurate than she was a year earlier.

By the age of five, most children have conquered many of their articulation deficiencies. Some children celebrate such conquests as did the boy who could not say "I" until one day he found himself saying "love" and "yellow" without difficulty. At that happy discovery, he made up a song, which he sang to himself, Pooh-fashion: "Yellow, yellow, yellow, it is so easy to say yellow." The questions asked by the five-year-old are less rhetorical and more to the point than they were a year earlier, and parents find them easier and more interesting to answer.

At this age, the child is becoming quite practical in her orientation and wants to know what things are for and what you do with them. This orientation is reflected in her definitions of words—"A horse is to ride, a fork is to eat, and a hole is to dig." The five-year-old is beginning to move away from the enjoyment of the kind of fantasy depicted in fairy tales but she will still sit and listen when a story of this kind is being read to a younger child. Her preferences, however, are moving towards realism and comedy and away from fantasy and magic.

The language proficiency of the five-year-old is truly re-markable and the conversations held by children at this age are a delight to hear. Here is an example from Gesell that illustrates the way in which a five has it over a four:

> Four: *"I know that Pontius Pilate is a tree."*
> Five: *"No, Pontius Pilate is not a tree at all."*
> Four: *"Yes, it was a tree because it says: He suffered under Pontius Pilate so it must have been a tree."*
> Five: *"No, I am sure Pontius Pilate was a person and not a tree."*
> Four: *"I know he was a tree, because he suffered under a tree—a big tree."*
> Five: *"No, he was a person but he was a very pontious person."*

The five-year-old often mishears many adult productions. For example, there was the Connecticut youngster who sang out in church: "Our father who are in New Haven, Harold be thy name." And many a five-year-old goes to church eager to see the hallowed "cross-eyed bear" (cross I'd bear).

In his social behavior, the five-year-old is clearly the capstone of the preschool period. She is quite self-sufficient in so many different domains that she might easily be taken for a miniature adult. She enjoys her own friends, whom she goes to visit on her own, chooses her own activities and TV shows, and is relatively undemanding of parental time and attention. More-over, five tends to handle stress in a calm and matter of fact way. If she gets separated from her parents, she will tell the policeman her name and address and may even enjoy the excite-ment of the separation.

The five-year-old thus reflects, in many ways, the bene-fits of five years of socialization within the family and nursery school. She tends to be socially outgoing, self-assured, and eager to go to school and to learn the academic skills of reading and writing. She also wants to go to school because it is a sign of being more grown-up and independent. She has grown with all that her limited world could offer and is now prepared to meet the larger world of school and community.

PART II

The Child

6 Personal and Social Development

The elementary school years, roughly from age six through age eleven, are in a sense an intermezzo between the rapid growth of the preschool years and the accelerated growth pace of adolescence. It would be a mistake, however, to think of childhood proper as simply a period of marking time until adolescence. In fact, much is happening that flows from experiences in the preschool period and that prepares for the onset of the next growth epoch. The elementary school child, by the very nature of his appearance, both reminds us of his past and suggests his future.

In general, childhood tends to involve a solidification of social patterns that were first evidenced in the preschool period. The child who is active and social and is an initiator of activities in nursery school continues to be so in the grade school period, but in more formalized ways. He becomes captain of his team, president of his class, and so on. Likewise, the child who is on the sideline of things in nursery school tends to perpetuate this role in the elementary school. Remarkable changes can and do occur, of course, as some children "find" themselves in school or, because of unforeseen circumstances such as a death or divorce in the family, change their pattern of interaction for the worse. In general, however, continuity with preschool social patterns is the rule rather than the exception.

The same tends to be true for patterns of achievement. By the age of four, one can make fairly accurate predictions about the child's intellectual potential that will not be fully realized until age sixteen or seventeen. Children who are bright and alert in the preschool will continue to be the good learners in the elementary school. The same will hold true for children who are relatively slow in nursery school activities. Once again, there are wide individual differences. Some children will make phenomenal gains in intellectual ability when they enter school, whereas other children who seemed bright with promise begin to show a gradual decline in intellectual achievement. By and large, however, continuity rather than discontinuity is the rule with respect to intellectual attainments during the preschool and elementary school years.

Finally, continuity is also the rule for physical attainments. Children who are well coordinated and who will be good at sports show their talents early in such things as catching balls, riding bikes, and performing other motor skills. During the preschool period the less motorically adept youngsters will also show signs of the difficulties to come in the area of physical activity. Here again, while continuity is the rule, individual exceptions are not infrequent, and preschool children who seemed clumsy may turn out to be quite athletically inclined. While athletic prowess is to some extent a matter of physical endowment, it can be improved with practice and the elimination of fear.

Facets of Growth and Development

Growth during the elementary school years is of many different kinds and includes physical increases in height, weight, and strength, increased sexual differentiation, increased intellectual powers for learning and problem solving, and vastly expanded social awareness and participation. Each of these facets of growth needs to be described in detail.

Physical Development

In contrast to the rapid increase in weight and height during the first months and years of life, height and weight increase much more slowly and evenly during middle and late childhood. On the average, most elementary school children gain two or three inches in height each year. There is apparently some relationship between the onset of puberty (sexual maturity) and height. Girls, who on the average begin puberty at age eleven, have an average height of 58.0 inches at that age, whereas boys, who do not begin puberty until a year later, have an average height of 57.5 inches at the same age. Put differently, there is a period, in early adolescence, when girls are taller and more physically mature than boys of the same age.

There is evidence that height is related not only to parents' height but also to such things as weight and intelligence. Thin boys are likely to be shorter, for example, than are heavier boys of the same age. Likewise, bright children are likely to be taller than children who are average or below average in intelligence. It must be remembered, however, that there are many exceptions to these relations of height to weight and to IQ. Some thin children are quite tall, and some short children are exceptionally bright. So, while the general trends need to be remembered, the exceptions should not be forgotten.

Just as growth in height attains a more steady pace in childhood so too does growth in weight. At the age of six years the child should be about seven times his or her birth weight. To illustrate, a child who had a birth weight of 7 pounds would be expected to weigh close to 50 pounds at age six. The average weight for six-year-old girls is 48.5 pounds, while the average boy weighs 49 pounds at age six. By the end of the elementary school period the average girl weighs 88.5 pounds, whereas the average boy weighs 85.5 pounds. At age twelve the figures are 100.5 pounds for girls and 96 pounds for boys. Here, again, it must be emphasized that these figures are averages, and that wide individual differences in growth rates—hence in height and weight at any given age—are as much the rule as the exception.

At the ages of five and six, children demonstrate rather finicky appetites and faddish attitudes towards food, but this tendency declines during the elementary school years, when healthy appetites are the rule. Some children, because of unhappiness or unfortunate parental models, may overeat and become obese. Obesity not only makes the child the butt of jokes and ridicule, it also interferes with active play and the attainment of some of the social skills that are acquired by interacting as a team member. The fat child will often try to buy friends and to accept the role of clown in order to attain some measure of social acceptance.

In addition to height and weight changes during the elementary school years, there are also changes in body proportions. Like the preschool child, the elementary school child has a head that is too large for his body. The adult's head is about one-seventh of his total size, whereas the toddler's head is about one-fourth of his body. This disproportion decreases gradually during the middle and late childhood years. In addition, the eruption of the permanent teeth and the enlargement of the lower part of the face change the proportions of the face and make it appear less top-heavy.

Changes in trunk and limbs occur as well. The trunk becomes slimmer and more elongated in contrast to the chunkiness of the preschooler. The chest tends to become broader and flatter, which permits shoulders to droop. Arms and legs, moreover, become long and spindly with little evidence of musculature. It is the thinning out of the trunk and elongation of the spindly arms and legs that give the elementary school child the "all-arms-and-legs," gawky appearance. The hands and feet grow more slowly than the arms and legs. It is the different rates of growth of different body parts that help to account for the awkwardness and clumsiness of the youngster in the late childhood years.

For the adult, who is reasonably well adapted to his body and appearance, it is often difficult to remember the child's sensitivity and concern about his body. The homely child or the one with a physical anomaly suffers untold agonies at the expense of his peers, who may tease or ostracize him from the group. Similar agonies are experienced by the child who is forced by necessity, or by unthinking parents, to wear clothing that is not in vogue or that is ill fitting or tattered. Although prejudice in the true sense has not yet emerged, children are hostile to those youngsters who deviate from the norm of dress and appearance and make them the butt of their anger and derision. In such cases the teacher can help by making the child's plight known to the parents and by communicating a sense of acceptance and positive regard for the child that his or her children can emulate.

Sexual Differentiation

Within psychoanalytic theory, the period from six to twelve, the elementary school years, is spoken of as the *latency* period. It is a time, presumably, when sexual desires are of no great moment. In fact, however, there is a great deal of sexual interest, if not desire, during the elementary school years. In addition, the elementary school years do bear witness to the gradual learning of sex-appropriate behaviors, attitudes, and manners.

Sex differences are seen most readily in play activities. In general, boys tend to engage in vigorous active play and highly organized games that require muscular dexterity and skill and that involve competition between teams. Girls, in contrast, tend to participate in more sedentary activities, such as cooking and dressing up. These differences, it is important to note, are heavily culturally conditioned. With the breakdown of sexual stereotyping, many more boys are engaging in cooking and sewing and many more girls are participating in team and competitive sports. In the future, hopefully, it will be interest and ability, rather than sex, that will determine which activities boys and girls will engage in.

Other sex differences can also be observed during middle and late childhood. Boys tend to show more dominant behavior and to be more quarrelsome than girls. The tendency for boys to be more aggressive than girls is also reflected in the statistics from child guidance clinics and courts, where many more boys than girls are usually seen. On the average, there are three boys referred to such agencies for every girl who is referred. These figures are not static, however, and recently many more girls than heretofore are manifesting behavior problems, particularly at the adolescent level. Again, cultural sex-role stereotyping is at work here.

One last area of sex differences that needs to be discussed has to do with mental abilities. Although the experts are not always in agreement in this area, it does appear that girls tend to be superior in verbal skills such as vocabulary and reading, whereas boys tend to excel in mathematics and spatial relations tasks. These differences are reflected both in intelligence tests and in measures of school achievement. Other evidence of the language difficulties of boys in comparison to girls is the fact that many more boys than girls stutter and manifest reading problems.

Psychological Developments

Perhaps the major psychological issue of the middle to late childhood period is the conflict between the child's desire to grow up and his desire to remain a child forever (a fantasy embodied in J. M. Barrie's Peter Pan). The child wants to grow up so that he can enjoy the prerogatives of adult life: the right to stay up late, to go for trips, to drive the car, and to wear adult-style clothes. More than that, the child wants to be big and to live in a world adapted to his size rather than the world in which he does live, where everything is several sizes too large for him. Finally, he wants to know all the adult "secrets"—the answers to his many questions about the physical world, about sexuality, and about interpersonal relations that adults tell him he cannot yet understand. He wants to be able to laugh at the jokes his parents laugh at and, most of all, to be accepted into their confidence and their "secret" discussions.

On the other hand, he also wants to be a child and to retain the many prerogatives of childhood. Quarreling, fighting, and roughhousing are accepted boy behavior, whereas they are regarded as rowdyism in adolescence. Likewise, the girl who paints her face and wears her mother's clothes is merely amusing, whereas such behavior on the part of her adolescent sister may be cause for alarm. Children are given toys as gifts, not just money or useful things (such as pens and pencils). They are still permitted emotional extravagances (climbing into parents' bed, pillow fights, and so on) that will later be forbidden.

In addition to the positive features of staying small, children see negative features to growing old. Adults often appear smelly (tobacco, alcohol), hairy (beards), and coarse (the enlarged pores of the adult skin, the facial lines, double chins and so on), which children find repulsive and against their aesthetic grain. At the same time that children want to assume adult roles and become privy to adult secrets, they fear these very same roles and secrets.

Other psychological features of this age period include fears and anxieties about academic achievement and social acceptance. While the preschool child fears animals and imaginary beings, the school-age child fears failure at school and rejection by his peers. It is because academic achievement is so valued by parents and teachers that it comes to be a focus of concern and preoccupation of children. Likewise, as the peer group comes to play an increasingly important role in his sphere of activities, acceptance by the group becomes an increasingly potent source of anxiety. Fears of rejection and failure thus emerge as prominent components of the elementary school child's experience and behavior.

Social Development

Adults frequently forget that there is a culture of childhood that is tremendously viable even though it is passed on solely by oral tradition. Children's games, such as hopscotch, marbles, kick the can, and blindman's buff, are passed down verbally from generation to generation. All sorts of jokes, riddles, and sayings, with slight modification, are also transmitted from generation to generation. In contrast to the culture of adolescence, which is constantly changing, the culture of childhood has considerable stability.

To illustrate some aspects of this culture of childhood here are some contemporary gibes that have to do with intelligence and appearance:

> *You make as much sense as an ejector seat on a helicopter.*
>
> *When you were born, the doctor spanked your face.*

But when they are called names children today may respond as they did centuries ago:

> *Sticks and stones may break my bones, but names will never hurt me.*
>
> *When I'm dead and in my grave, you'll be sorry for what you called me.*

Like nicknames, superstitions of children are passed on by oral tradition. On seeing an ambulance a child may chant:

> *Cross my fingers*
> *Cross my toes.*
> *Hope I don't go*
> *In one of those.*

Or, with respect to ladybirds:

> *Ladybird, ladybird, fly away home!*
> *Your house is on fire, your children are gone,*
> *Except the little one under the stone.*
> *Ladybird, ladybird, fly away home.*

Or with respect to rain, recall:

> *Rain, rain go away!*
> *Come again another day.*

One final illustration of traditional child lore. A child says to another, "Do, Re, and Mi went into the monkey house. Do and Re came out. Who was inside?" The other child replies "Mi," to which the first retorts, "Oh, I didn't know you were a monkey."

Children, in addition, often modify the older versions into contemporary idiom. A current version of the Adam and Eve and Pinch Me trick is the following: "Do you want a Hawaiian punch?" If the other child is caught thinking of the fruit drink and replies "yes," he gets punched in the shoulder.

The culture of childhood is traditional and rooted in the past, and this is a clue to the child's relation to the family during the elementary school period. In contrast to the revolutionary and often anarchic adolescent, the child is a staid traditionalist who accepts the authority of the family without question, just as he accepts the games and superstitions of previous generations of children. So the child is more likely to defend than to attack his family and what it stands for. The family is still the main base of security and identity and is still more important than the peer group.

As in the case of all who are tradition-bound, a certain rigidity is also noticeable in children. They are very much influenced by appearances and can be cruel to children who deviate from the norm of behavior. Youngsters who dress or speak differently or who have physical handicaps can often be cruelly treated by other children. Adolescents, in contrast, are more tolerant of superficial differences in dress and behavior but less tolerant of more fundamental differences such as those of religion or social status. The traditionalism of childhood thus has positive and negative consequences. Because the child accepts adult authority, he is tractable and relatively easy to manage. At the same time, the need for uniformity often makes him antagonistic to indivduals who deviate from what he regards as the general norm.

Sociocultural Change

Changes within society affect children less than they do adolescents. This is partly due to the fact of child culture, which is apparently little altered by changing events and circumstances.

Obviously, however, technological changes do affect children in countless ways. The pervasiveness of television and new space-age toys are bound to affect the outlook of children. It is not unusual, to illustrate, to hear seven- and eight-year-old boys discuss features of the latest spacecraft with the same expertise with which their fathers discussed automobiles. Likewise, toys such as model computer kits bring features of the space age into the home.

In general, the most noticeable effect upon children of the rapid rate of technological change characteristic of our society is probably to accelerate mental growth. There is some evidence that the overall level of IQ within the nation is rising. While this rise is probably due to many different factors, one of these is likely to be the early exposure of most young people to the world of science. Our children are, then, becoming more intellectually sophisticated at an early age. But this is a visual and experiential sophistication, far different from the scholastic sophistication (in Latin, for example) of early generations of young people.

One feature of contemporary society that is having a direct effect upon young people is the increasing rate of divorce. It is estimated that about one in three marriages in America ends in divorce. The effects of divorce upon young people are extremely variable and depend upon many different circumstances such as the age of the children, the quality of home life prior to the divorce, and the maturity of parents. One can say that divorce is always an emotional trauma for children as well as for parents. But the effects of the trauma will be different for different children. For some children it may be beneficial and they may grow emotionally as a result, whereas other children may remain permanently scarred.

Because divorce is becoming an accepted part of American family life, the stigma once associated with it has greatly diminished. This in and of itself makes it easier for children of divorced couples. In addition, the provision of joint custody, by which both parents, though divorced, continue to provide for the needs of their children, can lessen some of the pain of separation from one or the other parent. If parents do not use the children to punish each other and if they keep the welfare of the children in mind, divorce need not have lasting negative effects upon the children.

Other aspects of sociocultural change will also affect children differently, depending upon their socioeconomic status. Children in the suburbs are more isolated from the battle of black Americans for equality and justice than are white urban youngsters. A few black children may be bused into a suburban school, and suburban children may see a black maid or two, but aside from these encounters and the increasingly frequent presence of blacks in readers, on TV, in government and business, and in sports, they will have little direct acquaintance with the battle for racial equality. Children of less affluent families, however, who live in transitional neighborhoods in which there are large numbers of black families have a different experience. These children are made aware of the conflict of black and white society everyday, and this fact of sociocultural change looms very large in their experience.

General Characteristics of Middle and Late Childhood

It was said earlier that the child is by and large a traditionalist. He is also a pragmatist who is very much concerned with how things work rather than with why they work or with the evaluation of outcomes. It is an age in which doing, making, building are all important. Now that young people have good small, as well as large, muscular control, they are beset by the urge to sew, cook, and bake, and want to build, make, and put together. It is the model car and model airplane age as well as an age of cooking, knitting, and embroidery.

The child is an optimist as well as a pragmatist. One detects in most children a perennial cheerfulness that can be temporarily upset but that quickly reasserts itself. The world is a new and exciting place full of things to experience and to learn about. Because he lives in the here and now each activity is important and the most important activity is the one he is presently engaged in. That is why it is so difficult to disengage children from their play or work. Then too, because the child has so much to look forward to—that is, all the imagined joys of growing up—his optimism is seldom daunted.

This is not to say, of course, that children are always happy but only to suggest that their dominant mood is one of optimism. To be sure, children are upset by parents, by school, and by social failures. But the sense of hope is always there

—the hope that as the child grows up many of the problems will be solved. The child also has great optimism about what he can become and what he can do and is not bothered by the real hurdles in the way of attaining his goals. In fantasy the child can move away from the family, leave school, sail around the world and become a beachcomber or continue his studies and become a doctor or a lawyer. At its base, the child's optimism rests in his belief that he has an almost unlimited number of years to attain his goals.

A union of pragmatism and optimism in the child is not really surprising since the two usually go together. Those concerned with getting things done are often imbued with unlimited faith in what can be accomplished by persistent effort. And that is the true spirit of childhood.

The pragmatic attitude of children is very important for personality development and as preparation for the personality integration that is the task of adolescence, for by engaging in all sorts of activities, the child is discovering himself. It is a psychological truism that we are what we do. The child must discover what sort of pupil, athlete, musician, peer, and friend he really is, and these discoveries can be made only through his classroom work, his participation in sports, his efforts to play an instrument, and his interactions and friendships with peers. By engaging in these activities he evokes reactions in others that give him the information he needs to find out about himself.

Childhood then, is a period of self-discovery in which the child finds out about himself in the course of engaging in activities and relating to other persons. These various aspects of himself are, however, not yet coordinated into a general scheme of himself as a functioning totality. The child is more or less unaware of the various discontinuities in his behavior and in his self-evaluations. He may, for example, be a perfect gentleman at his friend's house but a demon at home or vice versa without being aware of the contradictions in his behavior. The adolescent may show similar contradictions, but he is aware that the behaviors differ and tries to rationalize the differences, at least to himself.

In addition to finding out about himself, the child is also discovering the larger social world about him, the world of entertainers, politicians, scientists, and athletes. Often children choose people from these professions as persons to idealize and emulate, particularly as they discover that their parents are not as all-knowing and all-powerful as they had thought. Parents are thus dethroned in the child's eyes, and new gods are introduced into the pantheon of childhood. However, it is often the glamour of the entertainer or athlete rather than his character or accomplishments that attracts the child.

This does not mean that the child denies the authority of the family, which is still the center of his life. It is just that other forms of authority begin to have an influence upon him, namely, the peer group and the new adult idols. The child's attitude to authority is not entirely subservient, for he does express his negative feelings towards adult constraint. He does so, however, in a manner peculiar to childhood—a manner that is often missed by adults. If one listens closely to children's rhymes and riddles, one notices that they often poke fun at important adults and at practices and institutions that adults take seriously. For example:

> Jingle bells, jingle bells,
> Nixon smells and Reagan ran away.
> Oh what fun it is to ride
> In a Carter Chevrolet.

Such gibes, it is important to note, are shared by the group so that no child takes individual responsibility for them. In this way the child can participate in hostile bantering of the adult world without fear of reprisal.

The dominant characteristics of middle and late childhood are, then, its traditionalism, its pragmatism, and its optimism. The elementary school years are devoted to discovering the self through repeated encounters with others and to discovering the world through incessant activity. While the child is generally subservient to authority he nonetheless expresses his underlying defiance in concert with the peer group and thus avoids taking any individual responsibility for being disrespectful to those who maintain the balance of power.

The World of Self, Home, and Community

The child's discovery of the various facets of himself leads to an increasingly accurate picture of himself and his traits. Children acknowledge their stubbornness, noisiness, and so on. In general, however, they often admit only to those negative traits, such as stubbornness, that are regarded with resigned amusement by adults. Traits that are regarded as being very negative are much less frequently admitted to, even though the child may believe they hold true for him.

Children's attitudes towards their parents vary considerably with the family structure. In general, children prefer parents who work together and cooperate in their child-rearing activities. They dislike parents who are arbitrary and who will not listen to their side of the story. While children appreciate parents who set rules and limits, they do not care for parents who are overly strict or overly lenient. Children interpret such extreme behavior, and often rightly, as meaning that the parents do not care enough about them. They see it as a form of rejection.

Within the home, the child's perception of himself and of his siblings is very much determined by his birth order. It is a well-established finding that firstborn children are usually high academic achievers even though their intelligence may be no greater than that of the other children in the family. From an early age the oldest child is expected to take some responsibility for his younger brothers and sisters and to be more mature for his age than his siblings. At least in part, the high achievement of the older child is probably due to parental demands for achievements beyond his years, which the child incorporates within himself. In any case, the oldest child is more likely than the children who come after to identify with authority and to adopt maternalist or paternalist attitudes towards siblings.

Effects of birth order in the self-perceptions of later-born children depend upon a complex of factors. It depends, for example, upon the age separation between the births, upon the sex of the children, and upon their relative intelligence. Apparently the optimal spacing of children is about two years. This gives the older child an appreciable time as the only or youngest child to whom most attention is directed without his getting a firm perception of himself in that role. When a child comes after only one year, the older sibling is likely to be more jealous than if the next baby came later. Not only did the older sibling not have the mother to himself for very long, during much of the time he did have her to himself she was carrying the baby and was often distracted.

In the same way, a baby who comes three or four years after the last child is also likely to be resented. The new baby

displaces the older youngster from a very comfortable and satis-
fying position in the family hierarchy. Obviously there are great
variations. In many cases the older child may be happy to have a
playmate after all those years or the parents may still favor the
older child. It makes a difference, too, whether the oldest sibling
is a boy and the next is a girl and vice versa. Like so many other
generalizations, those with respect to the effects of the age
spread between siblings have to be qualified by consideration of
all the possible variations and by the exceptions and special
cases.

    The middle child usually has the most problems, since he
has none of the benefits that accrue to being either first or last.
If, in addition, the older and younger side against him, his plight
is even more serious. In general, three is a bad number, whether
it be children or girls in a dormitory room. Inevitably there is a
two-against-one alignment, and the one person is ostracized.
Why this happens is hard to explain, but that it happens is easy
to demonstrate. The middle child in a three-child family is thus
likely to be denied not only a special place but also the support
of his siblings. Again, this generalization does not hold if the age
separations are great and the oldest, say, is many years older
than the two youngest or the sex distribution places the one boy
or girl in the middle.

    What is important to note is that the child's position in
the family plays a very significant part in how others react to
him and hence in the determination of his self-perception. If he
is the baby of the family he may always seek to be with older
friends so he retains his "youngest" status and may establish
other behavior patterns that will ensure that others will respond
to him in the same way that his brothers and sisters did. The
middle child, who may feel somewhat unwanted and unloved,
may work hard towards being accepted or move away from
people and become seclusive.

    It is imperative, then, in dealing with children to be
aware of their position in the family and the age separations between the children. This information often provides an important clue to the child's style and to his learning problems, if he
has them.

    Religious differences also color the child's self-percep-
tions, particularly among minority religious groups. Catholic
children soon learn of the long-standing prejudices in American
society against persons of their religion. Jewish children are also

likely to discover not only that they do not celebrate Christmas but also that they are "Christ killers" and "money lovers." Depending upon the intensity and frequency of such experiences, the young person may say, as one girl said to me, "I have the name so I might as well play the role," or he may try to be the opposite of the stereotype. In either case, the attitudes within the community towards people of the child's religion help shape certain aspects of his self-concept.

Other salient determinants of the child's self-perception are his ethnic background and socioeconomic status. It is simply a fact that any group that is in the minority will suffer lowered self-esteem. This is true whether it is black children who are a minority in a white school, or Jewish children in a predominantly Christian school, or Catholics in a largely Protestant school. Black children growing up in a predominantly black community in the South, for example, have higher self-esteem than black children growing up in northern urban communities. It is minority status, rather than ethnicity as such, that has a lowering effect upon self-esteem.

Social class differences also tend to shape the child's conception of himself and the world. Basil Bernstein, the English sociolinguist, suggests that the language of the low socioeconomic groups is *restricted* in the sense that much communication is by way of inflection and intonation. Among higher socioeconomic groups language is much more elaborate and specific. These different language patterns condition how parents and children interact and how they view or "frame" their worlds. In the United States, for example, low-income mothers use much less language when instructing a child than do middle-income mothers. These social class differences in framing the world are important. Recent research suggests that social class may be as important as intelligence and education in the determination of vocational success.

In addition to the direct effects of racial, ethnic, and economic status influences upon the child's self-conception, there are equally significant indirect effects. The values, expectations, and patterns of behavior of parents, varying greatly between economic groups, affect the child's school performance and hence his self-perception as a student. For instance, many economically distressed parents who are laborers or blue-collar workers do not prepare their children adequately for schools that are predominantly academic in their orientation.

Studies have shown that when economically disadvantaged mothers attempt to help their children solve problems, they often direct them to do the correct thing without explaining why they should perform as directed. Economically advantaged mothers, in contrast, are likely to offer lengthy verbal explanations such as "This goes in here because this is the box for the black buttons and this one goes in here because it is the box for the white buttons. Now, where does this button go?" The low-income mother is more likely to say "Put these in here and those in there."

Children who come from low-income families often lack, therefore, the extensive academic preparation for labeling, classifying, ordering, and comparing material and are likely to fail because the school assumes that these strategies of problem-solving and learning are already present. The children's academic failures due to inadequate preschool preparation often contribute to negative self-concepts and to learning difficulties. The situation is compounded by parents who want their children to achieve academically but who provide no evidence, in their own behavior, of intellectual interests or pursuits. Children do not respond well to the dictum "Do as I say, not as I do."

The child's perception of the home changes when he enters school. He learns from other children, and not infrequently from teachers, the social status of his family. He soon becomes aware of how his parents stand in the occupational status hierarchy. Children from homes in which parents have high status (fathers or mothers, say, who are in the professions or who own their own businesses or who are in high managerial positions) take pride in their family positions. Children, on the other hand, whose parents are blue-collar workers or skilled laborers may become ashamed of their families. Such differential perceptions are particularly in evidence where the social status of children within the same school shows considerable variation.

In considering the child's perception of the school, a factor in addition to ethnic and socioeconomic status must be taken into account. This factor is age. The young child who is just entering school is, in most cases, excited at the prospect. Going to school is, for one thing, a sign of growing up and evidence of increased independence. In addition, the child has heard a great deal about school and has high expectations about what he will do there. Unfortunately, this early enthusiasm for school is relatively short-lived, and by the time they reach fifth and sixth grade more than 50 percent of school children dislike school.

There are many reasons for this. An important one is the peer group, which sometimes takes an increasingly negative attitude towards school and which imposes this attitude upon its members. In addition, there are the individual experiences of failure, the inevitable personality clashes between particular teachers and children, and the interference of homework with desired activities. In the case of boys, there is another factor that leads to negative attitudes towards school. Boys are trained to be dominant and assertive with respect to girls but must be passive in relation to predominantly female teachers. For many boys this poses a real conflict insofar as it goes against their self-conceptions of masculinity.

The importance of the sex and attitudes of the teachers is reflected in data from Germany. There are more male teachers in Germany than in America for the lower grades. There is also a culturally determined attitude held by both male and female teachers: that education is more important for boys than for girls. One consequence of this situation is that in Germany there are more girls with reading problems than there are boys. This is just the reverse of the situation in America, where girls tend to be favored by teachers because they are more tractable and less trouble.

For a variety of reasons, therefore, the child's perception of the school changes from extremely positive to lukewarm or negative as he advances up the grades. While this does not hold for all children, it holds for a sufficient number of them to constitute a significant educational problem. Motivation is the single most important factor in learning, and dislike of school could well be one of the major hindrances to effective education.

By and large, the child has only a limited perception of the community as a whole. He knows parts of the community, such as its parks, zoos, museums, movies, and shopping malls, as well as some of its police, mail, and fire protection services. He has, on the other hand, little awareness of the more intricate functions of the local government and its politics, or of other public services such as mental health centers and social welfare agencies. Again, the child's relatively fragmented perception of the community will vary with social class. The lower-class child may be very well acquainted with the welfare agencies and hospital clinics. The middle-class child, on the other hand, is acquainted with private physicians and dentists but usually has no direct acquaintance with local government agencies. It is only towards the end of childhood that the young person begins to differentiate among local, state, and national governing bodies and services.

In contrast to the adolescent, who often sees at least part of his community in a negative light, most of the child's experiences tend to be positive. Firemen enjoy taking him through the firehouse and letting him climb on the engine. Since he is usually accompanied by parents when shopping, he is generally well received by salesmen in stores and by the caretaking personnel at parks and places of amusement. The Halloween trick-or-treat experience is still another factor in the child's positive view of the community. Towards the end of childhood, however, as young people are more on their own, they begin to come into conflict with neighbors and local merchants. Such conflicts are the prelude to more severe conflicts that often occur during the adolescent period. By and large, however, the child's perception of the community is a positive one, although he is acquainted only with limited aspects of it.

Let us turn now from the child's perception of himself and his world to the perception of the child by parents, other adults, and the community in general. Usually parents have a positive perception of boys and girls in middle and late childhood. While they are noisy and occasionally troublesome, children are, for the most part, obedient and relatively self-controlled. They do not demand excessive freedoms, and parents do not need to worry (at least in the majority of cases) about their smoking, drinking, taking drugs, or getting into predicaments related to sex. Children are still smaller than parents and do not as yet suggest that the parents are growing old. Nor do children challenge parental values or authority in any significant respect. For all these reasons, parents feel, for the most part, comfortable and pleased with their children during the elementary school years.

For adults outside the family, by and large the same holds true. In fact, most adults who have no children of their own seldom see children or interact with them except when they see them in passing on the streets, in the stores, or on the playground. When contacts do occur they are usually positive because children tend to be polite and well mannered with adults. While there are, of course, many exceptions to these generalizations, they would seem to hold true more frequently than not.

As in the case of adults, the community has little to do with children aside from providing educational and recreational services. Children are still the major responsibility of the family, and community agencies and administrative officers have little to do with them. There are exceptions, but these are usually children in trouble, or children who must be cared for in one way or another by local agencies. Aside from these functions and the community-provided activities such as parades or special exhibits designed particularly for children, the community's main concerns are elsewhere.

The Child in Relation to Adults

When we look at the interaction between children and adults in a general way, the most striking feature of these interactions is the inequality. Not only is the adult bigger and smarter, but he or she also has all of the power and authority in the relationship. It is the adult who dictates to the child and not the reverse. In many ways it is the inequality between adults and children that provides the clue to their effective and ineffective interactions.

Children, in order to redress some of the inequality between themselves and adults, often employ what amount to guerrilla tactics. We have already noted the hostile gibes and parodies on prominent adults and respected institutions. More than that, however, children become quite astute psychologists. They look for the adult's weak points and attack him or her at just those points. Parents, to illustrate, who are very concerned that their children eat well are likely to have children who show greater than average eating problems. Likewise, parents who are most concerned about what the neighbors think of their children are likely to have youngsters who misbehave in front of strangers. In a word, children discover what areas of their own activity most arouse parental anxiety and then engage in just those activities when they are frustrated or thwarted. Cartoons in which the "little guy" outwits the "big guy" are enjoyed by children because their view of the world is reflected in these cartoons.

Young people do the same thing with their teachers, but to a somewhat lesser extent. In general, children are less emotionally involved with their teachers and therefore much less bothered by the teachers' discipline and controls. Then, too, in the classroom the inequality of the relationship is balanced somewhat by the disproportionate number of children in relation to adults. Indeed, in the classroom it is often the group rather than an individual that finds the area of the teacher's anxiety. If the teacher is concerned about order and doubts his abilities in this regard, the group will discover this fact and test him severely. In the classroom it is likely to be the group and not the child that engages in guerrilla tactics.

There are exceptions, however, and when a particular child arouses great anxiety and hostility in a particular teacher there is cause for concern. What this means is that the relationship is more involved and emotionally charged than is healthy for teacher or child. When this occurs the teacher should talk the situation over with a sympathetic counselor or supervisor.

The ways in which children redress the inequality between adults and themselves are almost infinite. Some children throw tantrums or get ill and dominate parents who are afraid to control them for fear of another episode. Such children have their parents at their mercy. Other children engage in such destructive behavior that the parents are afraid to leave them alone with baby-sitters or even in another room. While such behaviors are attention-getting, they also serve to control parents. Other devices, such as failing to wash or take care of clothes, are characteristic of most children and have, in some degree or another, the intent of needling and aggravating adults.

One way children have of getting at their parents is by fighting among themselves. Of all child behaviors, fighting is probably the most distressing to parents. While fighting is an expression of many things besides an effort to upset parents, the fact that it usually occurs when parents are around is a good clue to its dynamics. In handling fights the natural tendency of parents is to take sides usually with the smaller sibling(s). Unfortunately, the younger may have been the instigator. If parents can keep their heads, the best procedure is to have each child "explain" what happened. What the children say is actually less important than that, in their eagerness to explain verbally, they forget about fighting physically. Asking for explanations can usually defuse the situation.

In summary, then, the relation between children and adults is one that is characterized by inequality of authority and power. Many of the disruptive and anxiety-provoking features of child behavior have, as one intention, the aim of partially redressing this balance. Children soon discover the area that their parents or teachers are most anxious about and choose this area of activity as a battleground. It needs to be emphasized, however, that while such retaliation on the part of children is normal and healthy, it can get out of hand. Children want to aggravate and provoke their parents occasionally; they do not want to control them. When, out of fear of what the child will do, adults let a child gain control, they are in for serious trouble. The child will use his power, even though he does not want it and is afraid of it. Such a situation is potentially explosive. So, while children should be expected to act against the inequality of the adult-child relationship, they should not be allowed to change the fact of that inequality, which is both natural and necessary.

Adults in Relation to Children

It was said above that the most general characteristic of the adult-child relationship is one of inequality. For the child in such a relationship, the problem is mainly one of how to redress the balance, and the preceding section attempted to detail some of the means used by children to do that. For adults, on the other hand, the problem is of a somewhat different order. The adult must learn how best to use the power and authority that is invested in him or her simply by virtue of his or her being a mature organism. Unlike other forms of authority and power, those we have over children are neither sought after nor won; rather, they are thrust upon us.

How then are we to handle our power and authority over children? There is no simple answer to this question, since people differ greatly in their personalities, their backgrounds, and their experience with children. What does hold true for every adult, however, is that he or she does have the authority and power and must recognize that fact. The parent or adult who tries to be "pals" with a child attempts to deny and abrogate the inequality of the adult-child relationship. Children like to play with adults, but such play should never be an excuse for the forfeit of adult authority, and responsibility.

Again, whatever adults' personal feelings and experiences with authority, they will utilize it better if they attempt to understand children on the one hand, and to think through what it is they want to accomplish on the other. This is as true for teachers as it is for parents. We need to understand the pressures, forces, fears, anxieties, and joys of growth that children are undergoing. In addition, we need to stop and think about the kind of child we want to raise and educate. We should have in our minds as clear a picture as possible of the sort of person we want our young charge to be. Specific techniques are less important than having a goal in mind, because the techniques often follow from the goal.

In this connection it is somewhat surprising that, in our highly specialized and technological society, we leave child-rearing to rank amateurs. Most parents today have little experience with children before they are confronted with their own and have little to guide them except what they learned from their parents. Probably our child-rearing activities are some of the least efficient aspects of our highly efficient society. Whether the solution is to have children brought up by experts or to make experts out of parents is not clear. What is clear is that a good many parents and teachers have the power and authority over children that is vested in them as adults but have no clear idea as to how to use this authority effectively. Perhaps the most important start in this direction, as we have suggested, is to learn about children, to formulate goals for child-rearing, and, finally, to maintain and not abrogate adult authority and power. But it should be said too that the most effective authority is that which is combined with warmth and compassion.

Parent-Child Contracts

In the foregoing paragraphs the child's position in relation to adults and the adult's relation to children were described. The present section will present a model for looking at the development of parent-child interactions.

One way in which the development of parent-child relations can be viewed is from the standpoint of the kinds of give-and-take arrangements that are explicitly or implicitly operative at all levels of development. At least three types of arrangements can be distinguished: the bargain, the agreement, and the contract. Each of these needs to be dealt with in a little more detail.

The simplest and most temporary parent-child arrangement is the *bargain*. In the bargaining arrangement, the parent offers the child some reward or withholds some punishment in return for a particular behavior on the part of the child. To illustrate, when the parent offers the child a treat if he will go to bed, this constitutes a bargain (not a bribe), a sort of one-shot arrangement. A child, at least a middle-class child, soon learns to initiate his own bargains at a fairly early age. A child-initiated bargain is illustrated by the following remark: "I'll get undressed and brush my teeth if I can stay up and watch the TV Special." Bargains change in their content as the child grows older, but continue to be viable means of socialization and interfamilial interaction.

A somewhat more complex, and more long-lasting, arrangement is the *agreement*. In the agreement arrangement, the parents and child agree to abide by certain rules over an indefinite period of time. Agreements with young children often involve the threat of punishment: "If you hit your little brother again you will have to go to your room and miss the cartoons," which can be translated as, "If you agree to leave your little brother alone we agree to let you watch the cartoons." Agreements at a later age level may become more positive. "If you clean up your room every day, I will increase your allowance." Like bargains, agreements change in their content as the child grows older but are present at all age stages of parent-child interaction. Whereas bargains appear to predominate at the preschool levels, thereafter agreements appear to become increasingly more prominent.

The most complex and least explicit parent-child arrangement is the *contract*. A parent-child contract consists in the unspoken demands made by parents and child upon one another that determine their mutual expectations. It is the sequence of parent-child contracts that most clearly reveals the developmental nature of parent-child relations. However, because contracts are mostly implicit and are seldom verbalized directly, their existence often comes to the surface only in the breach. That is to say, the existence of contracts usually becomes evident when either the parent or the child violates the contract. The mother, for example, who says "Look how they treat me after I worked and slaved for them" reveals her belief in an implicit contract, as does the remark of an adolescent: "No matter how much I do around the house, it is never enough." Such remarks, with which almost everyone is familiar, attest to the all-pervasive nature of implicit contractual arrangements between parents and children in our society.

The contracts written during the major periods of growth—infancy, preschool, childhood proper, and adolescence—all have particular contents characteristic of that epoch. In addition, the contracts at whatever age level also appear to have at least three invariant clauses—compensatory demands between parents and child. These clauses are the responsibility-freedom clause, the achievement-support clause, and the loyalty-commitment clause. In the following paragraphs the content of these clauses at different age levels will be briefly described.

During each of the four major growth periods, the parents demand that the child accept particular responsibilities while the child contracts for complementary freedoms. Parents generally require very little in the way of responsibility of an infant, and the infant, in turn, asks for little in the way of freedom. During the preschool period, however, parents begin to demand that the child take responsibility for feeding and dressing himself for bowel and bladder control, and to a certain degree for emotional behavior. Children, on their side, ask for some of the freedoms made possible by their new mobility and motor control. They demand free access to the various rooms of the house, permission to cross the street, and permission to handle tools and mechanical devices. In childhood, the responsibilities required of children become even more diverse and they are asked to look after their clothing, their rooms, and their younger siblings. Children in their turn, demand new freedoms in the way of staying away from home for longer periods and for going farther away from home. In adolescence, the contract is once more rewritten as parents request that young people take responsibility in the areas of sex, money, and cars and as the teenager asks for new freedoms in the way of late hours, dress, and friendships.

A similar developmental course is taken with respect to achievement and support. Parents demand little achievement of the infant other than that he walk and talk at the usual ages. The infant demands some emotional support for these achievements, but such skills are largely self-reinforcing. During the preschool period, however, parents begin to make demands for achievement in bowel and bladder control, linguistic prowess, and social behavior. For his part, the child asks that the parent praise his accomplishments and devote time to supervising and instructing him. As the child enters school, parental demands for achievement come to center upon the three major areas of academic performance, athletic skill, and social popularity. In return children make complementary demands for material, intellectual, and emotional support for their activities. During adolescence, parents intensify their demands in these areas and young people correspondingly escalate their requests for material, emotional, and intellectual support. Parents of adolescents are sometimes fooled, by the prominent monetary demands of this age group, into believing that their offspring are no longer interested in the more psychological forms of support. This is not the case and psychological support from parents is perhaps more necessary during adolescence than at any other time.

Finally, in the area of loyalty and commitment, a developmental progression is equally discernable. Parents usually demand little loyalty from the infant other than that he respond to them positively and with affection. Likewise, the infant appears only to request that the parents be committed to their caretaking function. As the child grows older the loyalty commitment clause begins to shift its focus. During the preschool period parents demand that the child maintain his loyalty and affection for them in the face of this exposure to new adults such as nursery school teachers and baby-sitters. The child, in turn, asks that parents maintain their commitment to him as new children are born into the family and as he makes new and greater demands upon their time and energies. Once the child enters school, parents generally require that loyalties to his family supersede his loyalties to the teacher and peer group. On his part, the child demands that parents give evidence of their commitment to him primarily in terms of the amount of time and interest they devote to his endeavors. In adolescence, this loyalty commitment clause takes on still another coloration as parents ask loyalty to their beliefs and values while the young person demands that parents be committed to the beliefs and values that they espouse.

This brief sketch of the development of parent-child contracts may suffice to illustrate both the age-related character of these contracts and the pervasiveness of the clauses regarding responsibility-freedom, achievement-support, and loyalty and commitment. Obviously this is a normative schema that holds primarily for intact, middle-class families in America. While I believe that parent-child contracts are written in families at all socioeconomic levels and in all cultures, the nature of the contracts and the invariant clauses they entail will necessarily vary in importance if not in kind for boys and girls and for different socioeconomic and cultural groups.

7 Mental Development

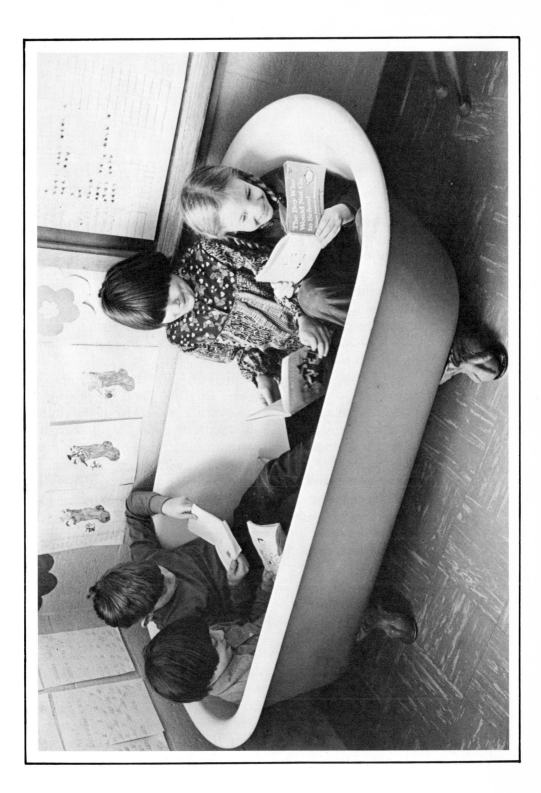

As in the case of physical and social growth, the growth of the child's mind shows continuity as well as change. The preschool child, to illustrate, has already acquired elementary concepts regarding number, space, time, and causality, as well as a multitude of other ideas, including conceptions of people, race, and religion. These concepts, however, are different from the concepts held by older children and adults. Put otherwise, the continuity in mental development resides in the fact that the child must struggle with the same intellectual problems during each growth period but with progressively better mental equipment and with correspondingly better results.

There is, it seems, a parallel between the progressive elaboration of an idea in the child's mind and the progressive refinement of a concept in scientific history. Among the Greeks, the atom was regarded as the smallest building block of matter. Later it was discovered that atoms, far from being single particles, are in fact miniature universes with a central core about which circle a variety of different elements. Both the Greeks and modern man have proposed a concept of the atom in connection with finding the irreducible elements of matter, but the atomic concepts of today are quite different from those held by the ancient Greeks. In the same way, the preschool child has concepts of space, time, and number, but these are quite at variance with the space, time, and number concepts of older children and adults.

In talking about the growth of the mind we need to distinguish between the growth of mental abilities (learning and reasoning processes) and the increase in knowledge acquired through the utilization of these mental abilities. For example, consider two boys of equal intelligence who grow up in different environments. One boy puts his intelligence to work acquiring knowledge in preparation for a career. The other boy put his mind to work to outwit the law and to devise schemes for fleecing unsuspecting victims of their money. Obviously many different factors operate to determine how mental ability will be used, and the point of the example was merely to illustrate that mental processes must be distinguished from their contents and from the ends they are made to serve.

In the following sections we will first review the development of various mental abilities and then look at the evolution of the products of these abilities, namely, the contents of children's minds. Put differently, we will look first at *how* children think and then turn to the question of *what* they think.

The Development of Mental Abilities

Any designation of mental abilities is bound to be arbitrary and to be objected to by some psychologists who hold a different conception of mental growth. This said, we will nonetheless discuss those mental abilities that would seem to be most important from an educational perspective: namely, perception, language, learning, reasoning, and problem-solving. Let us consider each of these in turn.

Perception

In the broadest sense, perception has to do with the ways in which we read the information that comes to us from our senses. We probably know most about visual perception, but we are also beginning to learn something about the development of hearing, touch, and smell perceptions as well. In addition, we are also learning something about the interaction of information that comes from different senses at the same time. We will deal with each of these topics.

Several general principles seem to hold true for the growth of visual perception. First of all, as the child grows older he is less and less bound by the physical organization or lack of organization of the objects or arrangements that he sees, and he can visually organize and explore them as he wishes. To illustrate, when preschool or kindergarten children are shown an eight-by-eleven inch sheet with familiar pictures pasted upon it in a disordered pattern they have difficulty in naming all the pictures. Older children, who are learning or have learned to read, have no difficulty with this disordered array. They impose their own left-to-right, top-to-bottom organization upon the scattered pictures and make no mistakes in identifying them.

Another characteristic of perceptual growth is that while the young child tends to focus upon a limited aspect of an arrangement or picture, the older child tends to explore the entire field systematically. When young children are asked to compare complex figures, such as two houses that are alike except for the number of windows, they say the two are the same if they find only one similarity without further exploration of the whole. Older children of seven or eight explore both houses completely before deciding whether the two are the same or different. Language enters in here of course, because young children understand *same* to mean alike in one characteristic. So the child's perceptual performance coincides to a certain extent with his language usage.

Not only do children explore their perceptual world more fully as they grow older, they also integrate and rearrange it more easily and more often. With respect to integration, when young children are shown a man made of fruit with an apple for a head, a pear for a body, bananas for legs and grapes for arms they name only the fruits and ignore the obvious man. By about first grade most children see the man, but then they ignore the fruit. By ages seven and eight many children integrate part and whole and report that they see a "man made of fruit." Turning to arrangement, as children get older there is a gradual increase in their ability to read things upside down, to unscramble words and to read run-on sentences (those without separations between the words).

During the elementary school years, then, perception becomes increasingly freed from the authority of physical configurations, and the child becomes increasingly able to find order in disarray, to take in all of the many and varied aspects of a configuration, to integrate parts and wholes, and to reorganize existing configurations into new organizations. The older child thus literally sees the world differently than does the younger child.

It is not possible to leave the topic of perceptual growth without mentioning reading. In recent years perception has come to be a favorite causative factor posited in reading difficulties. While there is no doubt that many poor readers have perceptual problems, it is probably a mistake to focus entirely upon perception as the prime cause of reading failure. Poor reading is a general symptom that, like fever, can signal a wide range of different conditions. For example, most children with reading problems have an emotional resistance to reading activities, based on their previous failures. Such emotional blocks can in turn affect perception. So while perception is certainly involved in reading, one should not place too great an emphasis on perceptual deficiencies alone, because it risks ignoring other equally important factors.

Language

Language is so intimately tied up with the growth of perception on the one hand and with learning and reasoning on the other, that it is highly arbitrary to treat it in isolation. It is nonetheless true that despite the close interdependence of language, perception, and thought, they are distinguishable and do not always run parallel courses of development.

In general, language tends to mature earlier than both perception and thought. Most children have fairly large vocabularies and have mastered the basic grammatical rules of tense, pluralization, and word order by the time they enter school. Indeed, children's grammatical errors (e.g., "feets") derive from the fact that children learn grammatical rules before they learn the exceptions. During the school years vocabulary continues to increase at a rapid rate and there is also growth in the child's ability to use complex and compound sentences to express himself. Although a few articulation problems (such as *f* for *th*) may still persist into kindergarten and first grade, most articulation problems are gone by the time the child reaches the third or fourth grade.

One aspect of language growth that needs to be mentioned is its progressive internalization. While young children think, they do so with the aid of images rather than by means of words. For the young child language is always outside and never inside the head. As children grow older, however, speech is miniaturized—whispering is a step along the way—until the child can talk to himself without being heard by others. There is a stage, it must be noted, when children have internalized language but still mouth the words. While this internalized language is not the same as thought, it does help to organize and direct thinking and does provide tools for use by thought processes.

Even when children have internalized language, they are still not aware of the fact that others cannot hear their internal dialogue. Hence, children in the early elementary school years tend to believe that adults can read their thoughts. They are often confused by adult demands to "tell the truth" because they feel that the adult can "hear" their thoughts. The young elementary school child's difficulties in keeping a secret arise from similar considerations. He doesn't take secrets seriously, in part because he really doesn't believe there are such things (and there would not be if we could read other people's internal dialogues).

While the pattern of language development sketched here probably holds true for middle-class children, the picture may well be different for children from low-income families. Language growth, to a much greater extent than either perceptual or thought development, is very much influenced by the models the child has to imitate. The growth of language ability is less rapid in homes where the educational background of parents is poor. In such homes there tends to be little interest in intellectual pursuits, such as reading, that would enrich the child's vocabulary and provide a wider variety of grammatical forms for him to copy. Consequently, many children who come from educationally limited families are handicapped when placed in a school setting geared, as most schools are, to children from educationally advantaged families. It should be said, however, that these children often learn a very complex and elegant dialect at an early age, and that their language "handicap" is only relative to the larger society and not to their immediate world.

The problem posed by language differences is that they are always confounded with cultural differences. A bilingual child is always a bicultural child as well. In teaching and working with bilingual children, such as Chicano or Indian children, the cultural differences loom as large as the language differences. In American Indian culture, for example, it is rude to look someone in the eye when you are talking to him or her. But in Anglo culture, just the reverse is true. One child was badly berated by his Anglo teacher because he would not look at her when he spoke to her. According to his culture he was behaving correctly, but according to her culture he was not. Teachers

need to become familiar with the cultures as well as with the
languages of the children they teach.

The relatively rapid evolution of language in relation to perception and thought and its great dependence upon parental models pose special problems for teachers. The sophisticated language of children from economically advantaged backgrounds misleads the teacher into assuming that their comprehension is on a par with their linguistic skill. This is far from being the case. For example, a very bright girl was always puzzled by the phrase "Once upon a time" at the beginning of a story because she could not understand how something could be "upon" time. She was so preoccupied with this and other metaphorical expressions that she often failed to enjoy the story. This illustrates how expressions that adults take for granted pose real problems of comprehension for children whose language skill suggests they do not have any difficulty with these expressions.

With children from linguistically poor or different backgrounds, just the opposite danger can occur. Because such children may have small vocabularies and poor grammar (at least from the teacher's point of view), teachers may grossly underestimate the mental ability of such children. One of my students, to illustrate, was tutoring a black girl who was regarded by her teacher and by the school as mentally retarded although she had never been tested. After working with her for some months, he so doubted this diagnosis that he tested her himself and found that she had an IQ of 125!

Learning

In general, we speak of learning when there is a change or modification in behavior or thinking as a result of some identifiable experience. There are, however, many different forms of learning or ways in which experience can affect behavior. Apparently, not all forms of learning are present at birth, and there appears to be an evolution of learning abilities just as there is an evolution in perceptual and linguistic skills.

Perhaps the biggest difference between the learning of preschool and school-age children is in the role of what is called *mediating processes*. A simple example of a mediating process is that of a young child who sees his mother put some candy away in the cupboard and then goes to find it the next morning before mother gets up. Clearly, the child had to store the information about the candy's hiding place in order to utilize it later. The ability to store information for retrieval and utilization later is one example of a mediating process.

While young children can use mediating processes such as language to a limited extent, it is not until the age of six or seven, when language is fully mastered and internalized, that language is used to help the child learn new concepts and relationships. For example, if a child is asked to remember a series of words or pictures that can be grouped in several large categories such as animals or fruit, the child who can group the specific items under the categorical words will remember more than a child who does not group the individual elements in this way.

Internalized language is but one of the new mediating processes that appear at about the age of six or seven. Other mediating processes are the reasoning operations we shall discuss in the next section. What needs to be emphasized here is that the emergence of mediating processes in the learning activities of school-age children makes for a remarkable increase in the proficiency with which they acquire and retain information.

Another change in the child's learning abilities comes about as a result of what some investigators have called *learning sets*. The notion of learning sets actually harks back to the ancient notion of formal discipline. According to the doctrine of formal discipline, one studied the classics, mathematics, and philosophy in order to develop the mind and not necessarily to learn specific content. The notion of learning sets is similar in that it proposes that if we have practiced solving a particular type of problem, not only have we learned the solution to the problem but we have also improved the proficiency with which we solve similar or related problems. Not only have we learned, we have learned to learn.

Learning sets are of obvious importance in education because our aim is not simply to increase the child's fund of information but also to improve his thinking abilities. It is well to realize, however, that learning sets may be negative as well as positive. It may be that a child who becomes extremely proficient at solving arithmetic problems with one technique may have more difficulty in learning new methods than children who have not mastered the technique as well. One of the dangers of increased proficiency of learning in a particular mode is increased rigidity of style and hence less openness to new and different modes of acquiring information.

As an illustration of how children can become "addicted" to a particular learning style, consider the case of Ross, an eight-year-old from Jamaica. When I first saw Ross he had never been to school and everything he had learned, he had learned by rote. Not surprisingly, he wanted to memorize everything, from math facts to spelling. But if he was confronted with a new word or new math problems, he could not decipher the word or solve the problem. It took a year of intensive work to get Ross to use analytic and reasoning processes as alternative learning modes.

An important, but relatively neglected form of learning is what I have called *connotative* learning. Basically connotative learning involves the re-presentation of experience. When a child talks about a trip he has taken, or writes about an animal he has seen, or draws a house he has visited, he is engaging in connotative learning. We engage in connotative learning whenever we try to put our feelings and/or thoughts into words and whenever we try to translate words into feelings and thoughts. Children need the opportunity to express themselves, and such expression is a form of learning.

Perhaps an adult example will help to make the concept of connotative learning more concrete. It has been said that the best way to learn something is to teach it. That is probably true. When we teach we re-present what we know. But to engage in such re-presentation we must make the material our own. If we know we are going to teach some material we approach it differently than if we just intend to learn it. Our approach is more active because we know that we must not only learn it, we must also convey what we have learned. In organizing knowledge so as to communicate it, we not only prepare to convey it to others, we also make it our own.

The importance of connotative learning is often overlooked at school and at home. I recall visiting a first grade classroom one day and watching a young man who seemed to be bursting with something to say, but could never seem to get a chance to say it. When I finally had a chance to talk to him and to ask if he had any news for me, he literally burst forth with "We have a brand new car with whitewall tires and blue paint and my daddy says I get to ride in it when I get home." Putting all that information into words is an important form of learning that needs to find a place in the classroom.

It needs to find a place at home as well. I suppose that I am as guilty as most parents of cutting my sons off when they want to tell me something of burning importance to them. My reaction often is "Tell me later, when I am not so busy." But later the excitement is gone. I try now, when I can, to attend when children want to talk, rather than when I want to listen. This isn't always possible of course, but it is possible more often than we would like to admit. Perhaps, if we realize that talking is a kind of learning—at least for children—we will be more willing to hear what young people have to say.

Memory

Three types of memory are generally recognized: recognition, recall, and reconstruction. Even young children are quite exceptional at recognition memory. After seeing a number of faces one time only, they can recognize them among unfamiliar faces without difficulty. Actually, recognition memory may become less adequate with age. Many children handily best adults at games like "Concentration" when it is necessary to recall the content and position of a number of cards that are face down in order to match pairs of cards correctly.

Recall memory, which is involved in remembering names, telephone numbers, and the like, tends to increase with age. Adults are able to learn poetry and the lines of a play more easily than children. It seems that this is not so much a matter of increased memory capacity as it is a matter of improved strategy. As we get older we learn a number of strategies for remembering things that enable us to learn and to recall them with greater facility than is true for children. For example, we learn to use mnemonic devices such as abbreviations (JFK stands for John F. Kennedy), and so on.

Reconstruction memory is the most complex form of memory, and the capacity for reconstruction memory does change with age. A child of four may not be able to tell you what he did the day before, because this requires a temporal and spatial ordering of events for which he does not yet have the concepts. As children's understanding of space and time expands, they become increasingly able to order their experience within these frameworks. Hence they are able to say what they did yesterday when their younger brothers and sisters cannot. Reconstructive memory is thus truly a reconstruction of past events that will vary in effectiveness depending upon the child's level of mental development and conceptual understanding.

Reasoning

Reasoning is the process of combining what we know according to certain rules in order to arrive at additional information. If we know that Great Danes are bigger than collies and that collies are bigger than dachshunds, we can, without comparing Great Danes and dachshunds directly, arrive at the conclusion that Great Danes are larger than dachshunds. Reasoning thus allows us to expand our knowledge by making us aware of the implications of what we already know. This is most clear in detective stories where the clever sleuth, utilizing the same information that is given to us, is able to deduce the identity of the murderer. Once the detective shows us which clues are important to reason about, we too can solve the crime.

Although young children employ a reasoning of sorts, it is a reasoning in action rather than a reasoning in thought. Young children can place a set of different-sized, doughnut-shaped, plastic rings upon a stick in a regular order from largest to smallest so as to make a cone. This presupposes the understanding of the relations A is greater than B, B is greater than C, and so on. But the child can do this only when he has the rings before him and can use trial and error to construct the cone. Reasoning is implicit in his actions but he cannot verbalize the relationships he has constructed.

By the age of six or seven, however, children can reason in their heads, and this is in part due to internalization of language. It is also due to the internalization of actions. The child can now perform mentally the trial-and-error activities that he had to perform before in fact. Given the plastic-ring problem, the child of six or seven surveys all the rings and mentally orders them as to size; only then does he proceed to place them upon the center stick. The same difference can be observed with pencil and paper mazes. The young child starts out and tries to find the path while drawing the line. The older child surveys the maze visually, looking for the correct path. Only when he finds it does he set pencil to paper.

This new capacity for reasoning displayed by the school-age child is shown most dramatically in the realms of class and relational concepts. With respect to class concepts, the child is now, for the first time, able to arrange them in a vertical order. Suppose we present a five-year-old with four red plastic elephants and two blue plastic elephants and ask whether there are more red or more blue elephants. The child will have no difficulty with this question. When, however, we ask whether there are more red or more plastic elephants, he will not be able to solve the problem and will again compare the red with the blue elephants.

To the young child a class is a kind of place, and since things cannot be in two places at once (the red place and the plastic place) the child cannot understand the problem. This way of thinking was epitomized by a five-year-old whom I asked, "Can you be an American and a Protestant at the same time?" to which he replied, "Only if you move!" To this young man "Protestant" and "American" were clearly places that you could not occupy at the same time. For the child of six or seven, however, a class of things is no longer regarded as a kind of place where all the elements sit. He recognizes that the same element can be in two classes at once. At this age children say without hesitation, "All the elephants are plastic, so there are more plastic elephants, because there are six of these and only four red elephants."

A similar transformation comes about in the child's reasoning about relationships such as *right* and *left*. If you place a preschool or kindergarten child opposite you and ask him to raise first his left hand and then his right hand, he can do so without difficulty. If, however, you then ask him to point to your left and right hands, he says that your right and left are opposite his own. For the young child, right and left are part of things, like their color and their form, and are not understood as relationships (such as *on* or *upon*) *between* things. By the age of six or seven the child has attained a relational conception of right and left and is able to distinguish between his own right and left arms and those of a person who is standing opposite him.

The development of these reasoning abilities makes formal education possible. Logic is implicit in verbal instructions, and much of what the teacher says to children presupposes a capacity to perform logical operations. When the teacher says that both *y* and *ie* can have the same sound he or she is asking the child to combine the vowel and vowel combination into a single phonic class. Logic is also required for elementary arithmetic, which is, in effect, the logic of numbers. The ordering of events in history and the causal sequences of events in social studies and science all presuppose elementary reasoning abilities. Logic and reasoning are thus implicit in all formal educational endeavors even though we are often unaware of their presence. When the prevalence of logic in our instructions to children is pointed out, we react like Molière's renowned character who was so delighted to discover that he had been speaking "prose" all of his life.

Problem-Solving

In the most general sense, problem-solving is a kind of one-trial learning. In problem-solving we bring our past experience to bear on a new problem, and often the solution comes suddenly, as the result of our seeing a new aspect or relationship within the situation. Problem-solving activity is present at all levels of development and can be observed in infants and young children. A young boy saw his mother place some candy in a high cupboard and wanted to get it. He looked about, moved a kitchen chair to the cupboard, and then climbed up and got the candy. Although he had climbed on chairs before, he had never before used a chair in this fashion.

In contrast to other types of learning, problem-solving situations admit of many different solutions. For example, the child might have used the shelves as a ladder to climb to the candy, or he might have used a broomstick to knock it off the shelf and onto the floor. Once the problem is solved the solution is retained, and the next time the child will use it immediately when he wants to get something that is out of reach. Adults solve problems all the time. Finding a way to get a cork out of a bottle without a corkscrew or to get a nail out without a hammer are common examples of problem-solving situations.

Proficiency in problem-solving probably depends in part upon past experience with similar situations. It probably also depends upon the child's creativity—his ability to think in novel rather than in conventional ways. Creativity, it has been found, is not the same as intelligence, and a boy with an IQ of 100 may be more creative than a boy with an IQ of 150. Many creative writers, for example, do not have exceptionally high IQs. In the physical and mathematical sciences, on the other hand, creativity and high IQ often go together, and creative problem-solving is at its peak in the period of early adulthood.

The Growth of Knowledge

In this section we will review some of the changes that occur during the elementary school years in the child's understanding of the physical and social world. First we will talk about changes in his ideas regarding quantity, space, time, and causality and then about his changing concepts of morality and religion.

Quantity Concepts

Among the most difficult concepts that children have to learn are those such as *more, less, same, all, some, few, and many.* These terms are difficult because they are used in such a variety of different ways and contexts and with respect to a wide variety of different things. The child hears such remarks as "How much more do you need?" "There is no more soda left," or "We need some more bread" and must interpret these varied quantitative terms.

Not surprisingly, the young child interprets quantitative terms with respect to actions. For example, a child is accustomed to hearing the word *more* in the context of his mother asking whether he wants more to eat or drink. Accordingly he regards any collection or amount of substance, to which an additional quantity has been added, as having "more" than another quantity to which nothing has been added. Somewhat later in the preschool period the child comes to judge quantity with respect to particular dimensions such as length or height. To see whether he has more chocolate milk than his brother a boy will push his glass next to his brother's and compare their levels.

It is only during the elementary school period, however, that children come to understand quantity terms in the same sense as they are understood by adults. A few examples may help to make this point concrete. If a preschool child is shown two equal sets of pennies that are aligned in identical rows he will agree that both sets of pennies have the "same number." If, however, the pennies in one of the rows are spaced farther apart than the other, the child will say that the longer row has more. At this stage, "more" means a single dimension (length) and not the number of elements. It is only at age six or seven that children understand that *more* and *same* refer to the *number* of pennies and not to the perceptual pattern of their arrangement.

This tendency of children to think of quantity in perceptual rather than in unit terms can also be observed with respect to length itself. If a preschool child is shown two identical unsharpened pencils that are aligned so that their ends do not overlap, the child will say that they are the same length. If one now pushes one of the pencils ahead of the other and repeats the question as to the equality of their length, a rather unexpected response is forthcoming. This child says that the pencil that is moved ahead is longer. Clearly, for the child, *longer* means *overlapping* and not *more units of length* as it does for the older child and adult. Once again the older child sees the length problem in unit terms so that he has no trouble in saying that the two pencils are of equal length.

A rather interesting development of quantitative concepts occurs with regard to concepts of substance, weight, and volume. This development has special interest because it shows in remarkable fashion the potency of the child's spontaneous concepts of quantity.

The demonstration is easy to arrange. All one needs are two identical clay balls and three children aged seven, nine, and eleven. Each child is tested individually and out of earshot of the others. We begin with the seven-year-old. We show him the two clay balls and ask him if both balls contain the same amount of clay. After he has agreed that both balls do indeed contain the same amount of clay, we roll one of the balls into a sausage in front of the child's eyes and ask whether there is as much clay in the sausage as there was in the ball. If our subject is like most children of that age, he will reply that both the ball and the sausage contain the same amount of clay and will offer one of three possible explanations: (1) Nothing was added or taken away, so they are the same; (2) What the sausage gained in length it lost in width, so the amount is the same; or (3) If you make the sausage back into a ball again they would be the same, so they must be the same now.

Suppose we roll the sausage back into the ball and ask our seven-year-old, "Are both balls the same weight?" Suppose, in addition, we make a small scale available to him so he can assure himself that they weigh the same. After he has agreed that the two balls have the same weight, we again make one of the balls into a sausage and repeat our question. This time, however, our seven-year-old reports that the sausage weighs more than the ball of clay "because it is longer." The interesting part of this response is that the child could have used the same arguments he used to justify the equality of clay in the ball and sausage for justifying the equality of weight between ball and sausage. But he does not do so because, apparently, his intuitive ideas about weight are not as easily overcome as they are about substance.

If we repeat the experiment with the nine-year-old child we discover that he judges the ball and sausage to have both the same amount of clay and the same weight. In justifying his replies, he gives one of the same three replies that were given by the seven-year-old. Suppose now, however, we again roll the sausage back into a ball and ask the nine-year-old whether both balls have the same volume or take up the same amount of space. After he agrees that that is indeed the case, we again roll one of the balls into a sausage and again repeat our question. This time the nine-year-old says the sausage contains more volume and takes up more space. Here again he might have evoked the explanations he gave for the equality of substance and weight between the ball and sausage but does not choose to do so.

It is only when we test the eleven-year-old that we find a subject who says that neither substance, weight, nor volume is affected by a change in the appearance of the quantity. Since, however, the child at age seven has the explanation for these equalities, why doesn't he use them? Why the delay? The reason is, apparently, that the idea of weight is more closely tied to certain of our actions (such as holding and lifting things) than is the idea of substance, and it is therefore correspondingly more difficult to overcome this intuitive idea of weight and to think of it objectively. The same holds true for volume, which is tied not only to our actions but to our internal experiences of "fullness" and "emptiness." The delay in the attainment of weight and volume concepts is thus due, not to a lack of the mental ability to think of them objectively, but rather to the difficulty in divorcing these ideas from our subjective experience.

These findings are not really surprising, since they demonstrate that intellectual ability is no guarantee of objectivity, something that all of us are aware of. Indeed, the roots of prejudice lie in the fact that the presence of reason is no guarantee that false ideas will be rooted out. In the case of the child, however, he does overcome his subjective prejudices and does eventually arrive at objective quantity concepts. Perhaps, if we knew more about how he overcomes his subjective biases we would have a better understanding of prejudice and of how to overcome it.

In summary, then, the child begins with rather different conceptions from adults with respect to such terms as *more, same, length, substance, weight,* and *volume.* However, as he begins to think of quantities in terms of units rather than in terms of perceptual dimensions, and as he gradually separates these concepts from his intuitive impressions of them, his understanding of quantity progressively approaches the objective ideas of quantity held by the adolescent and the adult.

Spatial Concepts

Space is a fundamental framework within which all behavior and experience occurs. The growing child must learn to deal with many different spatial concepts and relations. He must, for example, master *body* space and be aware of the positions, movements, interrelations, and coordinations of his arms and legs. In addition he must develop an understanding of *action space,* the immediate world of objects in which he carries out all the activities of his daily life. The child must also master the relations of *celestial* space (the world of sky, sun, moon, and stars) and become aware of *geographical* space (the relative position of land and water masses on the earth). Finally, the child must master *geopolitical* space (the geopolitical boundaries of states and countries around the world) and *representational* space, about the spatial relations represented in maps and drawings.

As one might expect, the child masters body and action spaces first, and only later and gradually comes to master celestial, geographical, and map spaces. It is during the elementary school period that the child begins to conquer these spatial aspects of the world that surrounds him. In each case, however, he first displays characteristic partial ideas that must be elaborated.

In regard to celestial space, the child begins, as did the ancients, with the belief that the earth is the center of the universe and the sun revolves about the earth. His first notions about celestial space also have an animistic quality, and he believes that the sun and moon follow him when he goes out for a walk and that clouds are alive because they move. Progress towards more objective concepts of celestial space come about as the child becomes progressively able to put himself in the position of other people and is able to overcome, by reason, the illusion of earth's centrality in the universe.

With respect to geographical space a similar development can be observed. The young child is not able to coordinate perspectives and may regard the same mountain or lake as different if he views it from a new vista. This has been shown experimentally with the following technique. A three-dimensional model of three mountains is placed upon a table, and the child is asked to walk around the table and observe the mountains from all angles. He is then seated in front of the model and is asked to choose, from several photographs, the vista that would be perceived by a child seated at different positions about the table. Not until advanced middle childhood can children succeed on this task.

We can observe a parallel growth from partial to elaborated concepts in the child's ideas about geopolitical or map space. Young children have great difficulty in imagining distant places, and "far away" is first understood in terms of concrete differences in clothing, language, mode of life, and shelter. Only late in middle childhood can the child think, say, of China in terms of imagined distance rather than in terms of sampans, Buddhas, and long coats. Similar difficulties are encountered when the child must deal with political boundaries. The young child cannot grasp that Chicago is within Illinois or that Illinois is within the United States and is more likely to think of these places as adjacent parcels of land. As the child's ability to reason and form higher-order concepts develops, he begins to grasp the true relationships between cities, states, and countries.

When we turn to representational space we again encounter characteristic misunderstandings in young children. To
illustrate, six- to seven-year-old children still draw pictures with
transparencies: that is, with features showing what would not be
seen in fact. A man on horseback, for example, is drawn so that
the line of the horse's body is seen through the man's leg. The
bottom half of a man in a boat is drawn within the lines of the
side of the boat. Then, too, when children are asked to draw a
picture of liquid in a bottle that has been tipped on its side they
draw the water level parallel to the bottom of the bottle and not
to the horizontal top of the table upon which the edge of the
bottle is resting. Equal difficulties are to be observed in the
child's attempts to master perspective.

By the end of the elementary school period, the basic
problems of representational space are mastered. Drawings no
longer show transparencies, relationships between liquids con-
tained in bottles and surfaces are correctly depicted, and perspective is used correctly. The conquest of representational
space, as is true for the conquest of celestial, geographic, and
geopolitical space, involves the use of formal operations, new
mental abilities that are acquired only in late childhood and
early adolescence. These will be described in detail in the
section on adolescent mental development.

Time Concepts

The child must master several forms of time, including psychological time, clock time, and calendar time. In the preschool
child psychological time is primary, and temporal intervals are
measured by the events that happen within them. This is the
only metric of time available to the young child, who lives from
moment to moment and event to event. To the young child
there is little difference between "later," "in a few minutes," or
"next week," which are all understood primarily as "not now."

The development of time concepts moves in two directions: to the minute divisions of clock time and the large divisions of calendar time. Preschool children distinguish first between day and night and then between various activities of their
routine day. By school age the youngster is on his way towards
the mastery of clock time, first by the full and then by the half
and quarter hours. Progress in calendar time concepts is somewhat less rapid. The child learns the days of the week first, then

months, and only late into middle childhood does he begin to appreciate years and dates. The understanding of calendar or historical time does not, therefore, come about until the child is eight or nine years of age. In fact, a true comprehension of historical time and realistic planning for the future does not emerge until adolescence.   •

A measure of the child's progressive comprehension of calendar time can be gleaned from the temporal words used in children's stories at various age levels. The preschool child's amorphous grasp of temporal relations is the reason for the vague "once upon a time" with which these stories are begun. Stories for later age groups begin to mention the seasons of the year and the days of the week as in books such as *Winnie the Pooh* and *Charlotte's Web*. But it is not until we come to books directed at young people in late childhood, such as *Robinson Crusoe* and the abridged *Gulliver's Travels,* that historical times are mentioned with any exactitude.

Causal Concepts

One of the major cognitive tasks of the school-age child is the progressive differentiation between *psychological* and *physical* causality: that is, between events that are dictated by human motives and intentions and those that are determined by physical laws or by chance. Preschool children do not make this distinction and often assume that physical events have psychological causes and vice versa. The infamous "why" questions of the preschool child must be understood in this light. When the four-year-old asks "Why do the stars shine?" or "Why is the grass green?" he wants to know their purpose and not their physical explanations. If the question as to why stars shine is answered "Because they are like fire," the child will not be satisfied, because he does not grasp the relationship between heat and light and because it does not fit the intent of his question. What he really wants to hear is something like "So that sailors can find their way at night."

It is equally true that the preschool child sees psychological events as having a physical cause. He regards dreams as coming in through the window at night and believes that prayers are made by God. He even believes that his feelings are physical and palpable to others. A young child once told me that he had a toothache, and when I asked whether it hurt very much he replied, "Yes, can't you feel it?"

As the child enters school and has an increased opportunity to test out his ideas against those of other children, there is a progressive modification of his causal conceptions. As a matter of fact, the child already has a fairly complex understanding of physical causality but now needs to translate this understanding into verbal comprehension. The preschool child, for example, knows a variety of causal connections as, say, between the light switch and the light going on and can operate a variety of toys that involve causal relationships. In the same way, he also understands a great deal about psychological causality and can associate his parents' anger with some action he has performed (indeed, may have performed to provoke that anger!).

These causal understandings are, however, intuitive and are not really conscious in the sense that the child could verbalize "The switch makes the light go on" or "Spilling my milk makes mommy angry." During the school years the child becomes progressively more conscious, or able to verbalize, psychological and physical causal relations that he has long understood. At the same time, however, in the face of new or frustrating situations he may revert back to the level of confusion between physical and psychological causality. Even adults do this and may kick the car when it doesn't start as if it were some malevolent enemy. Likewise, the "follow-through" of the bowler or golfer is often regarded as having some effect on the ball. This is a kind of confusion between psychological and physical causality that is retained into adulthood.

In the understanding of causal events, therefore, we see a complex situation. On the plane of action the young child shows that he can differentiate between physical and psychological causality, although he also shows many of the magical beliefs and actions that suggest a confusion between these forms of causality. The difference between the young child and older child is that the latter can verbally differentiate between physical and psychological causality, while the young child cannot. It is probably true, in addition, that the young child's grasp of differentiated physical and psychological causal relations is less broad than it is among older children, in whom this differentiation is more soundly based. Even adults, however, occasionally show remnants of the young child's tendency to assume that psychical events have physical effects and vice versa.

Moral Concepts

Morality involves a complex set of ideas, values, and beliefs regarding our relations to others that may or may not be related to actual behavior. Although we know a good deal about the cognitive aspects of morality, we have much less information regarding how and to what extent the child's changing understanding of moral ideas affects his actions.

In looking at the moral developments of the child we find two different orientations, one of which seems to derive from the child's experience with adults, while the other derives from his experience with peers. The orientation derived from adults, *the morality of authority,* tends to predominate in young children, who interact primarily with grown-ups. As the peer group becomes a dominant influence in the child's life the other orientation, *the morality of mutuality,* tends to predominate in the child's thinking if not in his actions. These two orientations lead to rather different conceptions of culpability of wrongdoing and of retribution and punishment.

Young children in whom the morality of authority dominates tend to be objective in their orientation to the notion of culpability. Children entering middle childhood tend to judge actions in terms of the objective damage done rather than in terms of intention. A child who broke twelve cups while helping his mother is regarded as being more at fault than a child who broke a single cup while attempting to get at a forbidden sweet. By late childhood, however, the morality of mutuality predominates and eleven- and twelve-year-old young people argue that the child who helped his mother was less bad than the child who was doing something he was not supposed to do. For these young people, intention rather than the amount of damage done is the main fact to be considered in assessing blame and in administering justice.

A similar development shift occurs in the child's evaluation of wrongdoing. Young children assess the enormity of a misdeed in terms of its size rather than its intention. To illustrate, six- and seven-year-old children regard a pupil who lies about his report card as having committed a less grave misdeed than a child who relates a fantasy such as having seen a dog as big as a horse. They reason that the child might have received the grade he said he did, while a dog the size of a horse is impossible; therefore the latter untruth is a more serious transgression.

Among children with the morality of mutuality—that is, among children in late childhood—just the reverse holds true. These youngsters say that lying about the grade is more serious than lying about the dog. The child who lied about the grade meant to deceive his mother, while the child who lied about the dog meant only to amuse her. Clearly they evaluated the act with respect to its intent and consequences rather than with respect to its plausibility, as was true for the younger children.

Parallel developmental trends can be observed with respect to concepts of retribution and punishment. By and large, preschool children have difficulty in distinguishing between an action and its consequences. They tend to think an act is bad or good depending upon whether or not it is punished rather than in terms of the act itself—whether or not it violates some rule or principle. In one study, children were asked to judge a helpful action (baby-sitting for the mother) that is later punished (the mother returns and spanks the baby-sitter). Before the age of six or seven, children said that the helpful boy was bad because he was punished; they failed to take his helpful act into account. Alternatively, some of these children attempted to fabricate a misdeed that would account for his being punished. Most seven-year-old children, in contrast, said that the boy was good even though he was punished. At this age, children judged an action independently of its consequences.

There is another aspect of the young child's moral views that is of particular interest because it occasionally appears in adults as well. Young children tend to believe that punishment automatically follows a wrong action. If something bad happens after they have done something wrong they regard this as punishment for their misdeeds. Adults, too, in times of stress may revert back to this notion of *imminent justice,* particularly when they exclaim, "What did I do to deserve this?" At such times the adult, like the child, refuses to believe that "God plays dice with the universe" and that there is such a thing as chance as a causal agent. Rather, they believe that it is a moral universe in which punishment follows only from a moral transgression.

A final dimension of moral development has to do with the relationship between personal inquiry and property damage. When intention is held constant, children at all age levels from kindergarten to sixth grade judge personal injury (say, a bloody nose) as more serious and more punishable than property damage (say, a broken doll). Young children say that a bloody nose "hurts" more. By second grade children express a kind of "cold cash morality" and say that a "bloody nose costs more than a doll." Finally, among the oldest children a genuine humanism emerges and they explain that "it is another person; you shouldn't hurt people."

In general, then, the moral development of the child during the elementary school years involves a progressive shift in his orientation from judging actions or events in terms of their seriousness or enormity to judging them by the intentions that motivated them. The child also learns to judge an action independently of its consequences and to realize that punishment and moral transgression are not necessarily causally related.

An important but difficult question is the relation between a child's understanding of moral ideas and his tendency to be moral in his actions. In general, the findings on this subject suggest that while there may be a relation between level of moral understanding and behavior the actions of most children are very much dependent upon the situation in which the opportunity for moral action presents itself. It may be, in fact, that children do not have a general concept of morality but learn about it only in specific settings. Their failure to behave at their level of understanding in new situations may, in fact, be a consequence of not perceiving the moral significance of their action in this new situation.

Probably the moral behavior of children is most directly affected by the behavior and teaching of the parents. If parents practice what they preach in the way of moral behavior, children are likely to follow suit. If, in contrast, parents tell children to be honest but are dishonest themselves, the children are likely to pick up the discrepancy and are more likely to imitate the parents' actions than to follow their moral precepts. The understanding of moral rules as to what is right and wrong is thus no guarantee of appropriate moral action, and this is as true for children as it is for adults.

Religious Concepts

In discussing the development of religious understanding in children we must distinguish, as William James did, between *institutional* and *personal* religion. Institutional religion has to do with the formal aspects of the church, its theology, and its sacraments and rituals. Personal religion has to do, in contrast, with the individual's response to the various aspects of formal religion. Psychologists are in general agreement that there are no uniquely religious motives, feelings, or ideas but that these elements become religious insofar as they become associated with elements of institutional religion. Put differently, personal religion is the individual's response to, and interpretation of, institutional religion and does not occur outside or independently of the church as an institution.

Personal religion, however, develops along two different fronts. One of these is *spontaneous* and involves the child's own interpretation of religious elements. The other is *acquired* and derives from religious instruction. Spontaneous religion is most prominent in young children and is gradually replaced by acquired religion as the child comes increasingly under the sway of religious instruction both directly through religious tutelage and indirectly through exposure to religious practices and participation in religious rituals and ceremonies.

The transition from spontaneous to acquired religion can be illustrated by the evolution of the child's understanding of his religious identity and by the evolution of his understanding of prayer. In both cases this evolution goes through a series of stages that are roughly associated with age. Let us consider first the evolution of the child's understanding of his religious identity and then follow his progressive comprehension of the meaning of prayer.

At the first stage in the evolution of his religious identity (usually ages five to seven), the child has only a general notion of the meaning of terms like Catholic, Protestant, and Jew. In his spontaneous attempt to understand these terms, the child confuses them with national and racial designations. A child at this stage will, for example, reply to the question "Are all boys and girls in the world Protestant?" something like the following: "No, some are Russian and Chinese." Likewise, when children at this stage are asked what a Protestant is they often reply "a man," and if asked how a Protestant is different from a Jew they might reply, "Because some people have black hair and some people have white hair." Furthermore, children at this stage believe that having a religious identity is incompatible with other identities and say that they cannot be Americans and Protestants, at the same time.

At the second stage (usually ages seven to nine) in the

understanding of religious identity children show some transitional ideas halfway between their spontaneously elaborated
meanings of religious terms and the meaning is generally
accepted by adults. When asked if all boys and girls in the world
are Protestant they reply, "No, because I know a boy who is
Catholic." By this stage children relate their own religious
denominations to other such denominations and no longer confuse them with national and racial concepts. In addition, they
now think of their religious denominations in terms of particular
appropriate actions ("A Protestant goes to a Protestant church")
and grasp that they can be both American and Protestant at the
same time.

At the third stage (usually ages nine to twelve) children's
understanding of their religious denominations is entirely acquired, in the sense that it is in close accord with the conceptions taught by institutional religion. It is a more abstract conception in the sense that the child now thinks in terms of general
categories rather than in terms of particular experiences or actions. At this stage the young person says that not all boys and
girls in the world are Protestant because "there are different reli-
gions in the world" and a Protestant is one who "believes in
Christ but not in the Pope." The question of being an American
and Protestant at the same time is dismissed with the remark
that "they are different things; one is your country, the other is
your religion."

The evolution from spontaneous to acquired conceptions of religious identity holds equally true for Protestant,
Catholic, and Jewish children, although there are some differences. Protestant children at the first stage are frequently confused about the notion of Protestant and its relation to terms
such as Congregationalist, Presbyterian, and Lutheran. Catholic
and Jewish children, who do not have this wealth of sects and
general terms to confuse them, are aware of their denominations
earlier and are somewhat clearer about them. This difference is,
however, erased by the second stage, when children can deal
with the relations between Protestantism and its subdivisions.

The child's understanding of prayer manifests roughly
the same developmental stages. At the first stage (usually ages
five to seven) children regard prayer as *asking* God for things.
(God is thought of by young children as an old man with a
beard.) Children at this stage usually ask for things such as

candy or toys for themselves. If prayers are not answered they "get mad" or "yell and scream" or "get angry at God."

At the second stage (usually ages seven to nine) prayer is understood as talking to God as well as asking Him for things, and He is thought of more in terms of His attributes, such as goodness, or as a creator. Seven- to nine-year-old children pray not only for themselves but also for their families and for their pets. If their prayers are not answered they are disappointed but look for reasons why this was the case — they were not good, and so on.

At the third stage (usually ages nine to twelve) children begin to understand prayer as a kind of private communication. Correspondingly, God at this stage is personalized and is thought of in such terms as "Master" or "Father." Now the child's prayers become altruistic and general, and he prays for "peace on earth" and for "food for the needy children." If his prayers are not answered the third-stage child argues that God can only help him realize his prayers but that he shares some responsibility for their fulfillment.

In general, then, both for religious denomination and for prayer, the child's religious understanding moves from a spontaneous, concrete, and confused notion to one that is acquired, abstract, and clearly in conformity with those of institutional religion.

These, then, are some aspects of the development of mental abilities and ideas during the elementary school years. While this is only a limited sampling of the child's broadening understanding of the physical and social world about him, it may suggest not only how much the child must learn but also how much he must unlearn. The growth of understanding is always a modification or reconstruction of previously held notions and is never a simple addition of new information. Moreover, a review of the child's ideas about the world indicates how great a gap, at least initially, there is between the adult's and the child's conception. If we wish to communicate with children we need to put ourselves in their position and view the world from their perspective. Knowing about the mental growth of the child is a necessary first step for understanding the world as the child sees it.

8 Age Profiles

In talking about children from six to eleven, we will focus first upon some general behavioral traits of the age period and then discuss the self-concept, social relations, and school orientation characteristic of that age group.

The Six-Year-Old

One of the general characteristics of the six-year-old child is high activity. Looking in on a first-grade class with the constant motion, jiggling, shoving, pushing, and talking can give the observer a distinct experience of seasickness. Whether sitting or standing, six wiggles and squirms. Six makes faces, imitates the latest dances he has seen on TV, and is constantly bouncing out of his chair, even during the evening meal. There is a lot of boisterous play and verbal aggression. Phrases such as "you stink" or "you are funny looking" are frequent. At this age, however, the child may be more ready to dish it out than to receive it and is sensitive about being called the names he so readily calls others. While he likes to roughhouse, he may not know when to stop and may get hurt.

By the age of six, children are interested in games with rules, which can be played by several children or adults. Games with spinners, wherein each child takes his turn, are popular, as are simple motor games such as knock hockey. Most six-year-old children are able to ride a two-wheeler and handle it well. Although children at this age attempt checkers and chess, they are not too good at these games yet, and even ticktacktoe gives them some difficulty. Played well, these games require strategy and foresight, both of which are not highly developed at age six. Making things — for example, toy boats out of pieces of wood or paperweights out of painted stones — are high on the six-year-old's list of preferred activities.

The six-year-old tends to be clumsy and a dawdler. Parents often have to fight to get him dressed to go to school or other places. On his side, however, he wants things done at once and gets upset if the adult does not drop everything and do his bidding. In activities, as in play, he may not know when to stop and may exhaust himself and then get angry. The same holds true for his insatiable taste for sweets, which often leads him to awaken before his parents and ransack the house in search of candy, which he may then eat in large amounts. Six, in fact, is almost always eating, particularly after school.

The six-year-old needs to be at the center of things, to be first, and to win. He is seldom modest about his accomplishments and may exclaim, "I'm pretty good, aren't I!" At this age he is assertive, bossy, and extremely sensitive to real or imagined slights. He feels he is being treated unfairly if a sibling gets a present and he doesn't, and he gets upset if someone gets more than he does, although he does not complain about receiving the lion's share himself. He is very free with opinions and advice, whether or not they are asked for, and imposes his wants upon his parents without any recognition of the fact that they may be involved in some other activity that precludes their interacting with him. It is not unusual for a six-year-old to ask a parent to play a game while the parent is eating his or her supper.

During this age period the child begins to differentiate his self-concept by putting himself in opposition to his mother (this is true for girls as well as boys), sometimes calling her names ("stupid idiot," "I hate you," "mean"). At other times he may say, "I love you" and write her notes and make her presents. The strain of growing up and being a school child sometimes shows in periods of regression, when six may engage in baby talk in imitation of his younger brothers and sisters and may even engage in some babyish behaviors. Because six is now in school and exposed to new values and standards, he is in somewhat of a turmoil of adaptation, which is a prelude to the similar but more intense turmoil he will manifest in early adolescence.

The six-year-old can give his parents a hard time, but, fortunately, it is not as incessant as the difficulties posed, say, by the two-year-old. At this stage he tends to be a know-it-all, which can grate on parents' nerves. The situation is not helped by the six-year-old's adverse reaction to criticism. In contrast to this assertive position, the six-year-old can also be affectionate and loving. Father is, if not the preferred parent at this stage, at least the one towards whom the child shows the more consistently positive attitude. Six-year-olds like to go places and do things with their fathers.

Relations with other children in the family are often competitive but will vary with the child's position in the family. If he is the oldest he may resent his younger brothers or sisters for getting into his things, and he is not above punching or pushing them for it. Occasionally, he may play with younger siblings, but he prefers children of his own age. If he has older siblings he may want to tag along and do the things his older brother or sister does. Although he wants to play games with his older siblings, he does not like to lose and may be discouraged from attempting them again.

With respect to peers, six-year-olds often pair up and have best friends with whom they spend a good deal of time. Such pairs often seem to take pleasure in ostracizing a third child who wants to join them. Friendships are rather erratic, and the combinations of pairs may change many times in the course of a year. There is also a lot of indelicate tattling and putting down of other children ("He didn't even know that"). Six-year-olds often say that they have boy or girl friends, and these are usually children in their school class whom they admire. While boys and girls occasionally play together at this age, the movement towards like-sexed friends has already begun.

The six-year-old has a positive attitude towards school and wants to attend, although he may decide otherwise by the end of the year. Even though six may like school, he occasionally, and sometimes frequently, decides he does not want to go. This may have to do with the events going on at school that day or with a transient desire to stay home with mother or to watch television. In part, too, the desire to stay home may reflect that being in school both morning and afternoon is tiring for a restless six-year-old, who may feel he needs a respite. Because going to school has not yet become a habit or a virtue the six-year-old does not feel guilty about staying home as he may when he gets older and school becomes something that is the "right" thing to do.

In general, a class of six-year-olds varies markedly from day to day in its level of activity and can be hectic one day and almost somnambulent the next. Children at this age like to work, but they work best in spurts and do not show the persistence they will later. Nonetheless, six-year-olds learn a good deal, particularly in the areas of reading and arithmetic. Most children enter first grade with only a knowledge of the alphabet and leave it with the ability to read through several primers. In the same way, children in the first grade also master elementary addition and subtraction. They make characteristic errors in reading and arithmetic, to be sure, but if these errors are not emphasized, and the thrust of their reading and number activities is encouraged, the errors will disappear of themselves as the child becomes more practiced and experienced.

The six-year-old child likes to bring home evidences of his schoolwork, such as his work papers and primers. He takes pride in the gold stars pasted on the work papers and attempts to explain away his occasional errors with such phrases as "I thought she meant plus but she wanted us to minus." Parental praise of these achievements is very highly valued, and a six-year-old can be shattered if the parent dismisses the work lightly or is derogatory about it. In contrast to his eagerness to impart his accomplishments at school to his parent, the six-year-old seldom tells about what happened at school and dismisses the question lightly if it is asked. He is less reticent in talking about schoolmates who do funny things or are outstanding in other regards.

In general, then, six is an active, outgoing age in which the child is basically self-centered. His own activities and pleasures take precedence over everything else. His self-centeredness has a certain charm, however, because he is not vain about accomplishments he can take no credit for, such as his looks, but is rather proud of what he has actually accomplished, and that sort of vanity is easier to accept and appreciate. He is still not a fully adapted school being and absences may be frequent, but he nevertheless gets a considerable amount of basic skill learning accomplished.

The Seven-Year-Old

Growth is never a regular process moving by equal increments like the hours of the day. Rather, growth shows periods of rapid activity and periods of relative quiet. Children need time to assimilate and integrate new experiences with which they have been bombarded. In this connection I recall visiting a railroad yard with a group of nursery school children. At the yard they climbed in the engine as it revolved on the turntable, pulled the whistle, and walked through the caboose. On the way home, however, all they talked about was the soft drink they had had as a snack. It was not until weeks later that they spontaneously began to draw railroad trains and to talk about their experience at the railroad station. Something similar happens at later age levels as well.

Towards the end of the seventh year and the beginning of the eighth, children begin to assimilate the wealth of new experiences to which they were opened in first grade. This attempt at digesting the experiences is seen in the relative quietness of seven-year-old children in contrast to their behavior at age six. It is as if their experience in first grade was comparable to the trip to the railroad yard; it needed time and work to become part of them. Age seven appears to be the period during which this digestive work is done.

In part, the reflectiveness and seriousness of the seven-year-old is attributable to the consolidation of the reasoning abilities that were used at age six to acquire information. These same abilities at age seven are used in addition to sift and sort information into categories and to relate the bits of information she has acquired. The course of this assimilation process is not always smooth, and the seven-year-old will show moods of brooding, pensiveness, sadness, and negativism. In a sense, one might even say that while at age six the child's activities were physical and motor, at age seven they become increasingly mental. It is not that the seven-year-old is less active than she was at six but rather that the scene of action has shifted and now takes place within her mind rather than within her action space.

The increased inwardness of the seven-year-old carries with it an increased sense of self and a heightened sensitivity to the reactions of others. Shame is a common emotion at this age and often centers about the child's body, which she does not like to expose or have touched. Because body self and psychic self are so close at this stage, we see a parallel reluctance to expose her ego to failure and criticism. Seven may often leave the scene rather than put herself in a position where she might be the center or object of criticism or disapproval.

It is important to emphasize, however, that the sensitivity of the seven-year-old is to what other children, her parents, and her teachers say and do and not to what they think. It is not until adolescence that young people can distinguish between what people say and do and what they are actually thinking. For age seven, saying, thinking, and doing are the same.

Perhaps because of her sensitiveness, seven often complains about having been treated unfairly and worries about people liking her. This concern is aided and abetted by the experience in first grade during which she attempted academic subjects and was rated against her peers on such things as reading ability, paying attention, and deportment. Not surprisingly, the seven-year-old manifests concern in just those areas on which the school, teachers, and parents choose to evaluate her publicly. It takes time for a child to assimilate these evaluations, which are quite different in content, but not in impact, from similar comparisons made by parents and strangers between the child and her brothers and sisters.

The relatively subdued quality of the seven-year-old has very positive consequences for her interpersonal relations. She is no longer the scourge of the dinner table that she was at the age of six when she bounced up and down, filled her mouth over-full, and ate with her fingers. Now she can listen instead of trying to do all the talking. She is, moreover, interested in being helpful around the house and asks to be given responsibilities such as running errands, helping to prepare dinner, or assisting her father in some work around the house. Finally, the child of seven shows a politeness and consideration towards adults that was seldom to be observed in the stormy petrel of a year earlier.

Although the seven-year-old may relate better to her siblings than she did at six, this relationship will depend upon how many they are and the age separations between them. In general, the closer the brothers and sisters are to her in age, the greater the likelihood of quarrels, fights, and bickering. Friendliness of relations seems to increase with the difference in ages among the children. At age seven the child still has a good time with friends but also enjoys solitary activities such as watching television, reading, and writing. When she is with older children and they are active and boisterous, the seven-year-old seems to have a better understanding of the situation and a greater ability to stop before things go too far and someone is hurt.

In her school life, the seven-year-old often shows an increased concern with the teacher and his or her response to her. This, again, may result from the evaluative experience she went through at age six. Similarly, the seven-year-old is not as interested in taking her work home as she was at age six and has lost her confident optimism in being able to do everything well. In some ways, the seven-year-old is more demanding of the teacher in that she is always asking questions such as "What do we do now?" and "How do we do this?" She is less sure she knows how to do everything before she is told and now begins to grasp the role of the teacher as a guide and model for her learning rather than as a mere stimulant to action.

The seven-year-old is more careful and persistent in her work habits than she was at age six. She likes to know where things begin and where they end and how far she is supposed to go, whether in reading, doing workbook exercises, or building something. Her reading and arithmetic skills are increasing apace, and she may begin reading all sorts of books, including comic books (many of which are, by the way, a fine, relatively harmless stimulant to reading interest). Reading errors are less frequent, her reading is more fluent and rapid, and she tries to maintain her speed by skipping or guessing at words she doesn't know rather than stopping to spell them out. By age seven she has already acquired a concern with the adequacy of her performance and wants to know immediately how well she has performed.

The seven-year-old is, then, while by no means a passive youngster, more serious, less talkative, and less impulsive than she was at age six and more sensitive to how other people react to her. At home she is tractable, polite, and eager to take on responsibility, although she can also be complaining and pensive. While she enjoys playing with friends, she also takes pleasure in solitary pursuits. At school she is a serious student, makes many demands upon teachers for assistance, and is concerned about the success of her performance. At this age she knows she is being evaluated and becomes particularly concerned about those areas of activity that schools, teachers, and parents choose to evaluate.

The Eight-Year-Old

The inward pensiveness of the seven-year-old as he takes time to consolidate his gains and integrate his varied experiences paves the way for a new outwardness as the child moves forward to his ninth year. The eight-year-old begins to seek new experiences, and his mood and style are active and expansive. His moving towards people and new experience is, however, more mature than it was in earlier periods, such as age four, when a similar mood prevailed. His interactions with adults are more productive, and he is more attentive and responsive to adult communications than he was at seven.

One new characteristic of the eight-year-old is his judgmental attitude. Perhaps in response to the open evaluations that are made of him by schoolteachers and parents, he adopts an appraising attitude in defense. Among clinicians such behavior is called "identifying with the aggressor." A child, for example, who comes home from the dentist and tries to poke sticks into his little brother's mouth is taking the role of the dentist. In this way, by being the aggressor rather than the aggressed-upon, he is able to cope with the anxiety-provoking experience of the dental chair. At age eight the child begins to judge and appraise what happens to him and to be concerned with the "why" of events.

There is at age eight a noticeable separation between the sexes. Boys are beginning to engage in group games that exclude girls. In addition, groups of boys may shout at groups of girls and tease them by chasing them on the playground and on the streets. The boy-girl separation at age eight is far from being complete, but the number of times that such separations and confrontations occur between boys and girls is larger than it was before. We see in the eight-year-old's attitude towards members of the opposite sex a combination of attraction and hostility, a pattern that will be seen again in early adolescence.

Another characteristic of the eight-year-old is his enormous curiosity. He has discovered how much there is to know in the world and has tasted the pleasure of discovery. He collects any number of different things, as any routine examination of the contents of his pockets and bureau drawers will readily reveal. Catalogues of large department stores are of particular interest, because of the many different things that are depicted. At age eight the child wants money to buy things and likes to barter and bargain. Children vary in their skill at trading, and some shrewd children may, from clever dealing, have quite a warehouse of toys, bikes, and books.

The eight-year-old's curiosity does not end with nature and man-made things; it extends to people as well. This interest in other people is shown in his attentiveness to adult discussions and his eagerness to observe at adult gatherings, such as parties given by his parents. At this age children also begin to evince interest in children from foreign lands and delight in learning that they do similar things. (Children, and even adults, often assume that something foreign is automatically not only different but also more primitive. Perhaps these assumptions are made because children are usually presented with the quaint, peasant aspect of foreign children and not with the life of city children. It often comes as a surprise to children and adults to find that people from other cultures have washing machines, cars, and elevators.)

In addition to his interest in foreign lands he has a comparable interest in earlier times — in Indians, knights, and even the Pilgrim fathers. The eight-year-old's concept of historical time is still qualitative in the sense that it is dependent upon physical attributes such as clothing to distinguish between different historical epochs. Nonetheless, he has gone beyond the primarily here-and-now orientation of earlier age periods and now thinks beyond the boundaries of his immediate time and space experiences.

To summarize, then, the eight-year-old shows a renewed interest and curiosity in the world about him. He is also more judgmental of his experience and of others and wants to know the why of things and social relations. His interests go beyond the immediate here and now; he finds the stories of foreign places and children enchanting and is beginning to be excited about historical events and peoples.

If we now look at the eight-year-old child's self-concept in more detail, we find notable advances beyond the previous stage. Eight has more self-confidence, perhaps because of his identification with adults and greater self-awareness. He is, moreover, as curious about himself as he is about other people and nature. Since self-awareness is largely derived from the reaction of other people towards us, the eight-year-old is constantly trying himself out on other children and adults. This increased differentiation of the self is evidenced in the child's use of the term *self*, which suggests that he is now judging and appraising himself as well as others. The eight-year-old's increased maturity in this regard is also observed and remarked upon by parents, who begin to note distinctive patterns of behavior and traits and remark "That's Bobby" or "That's Nancy" in response to a movement, expression, or remark.

Another way in which the eight-year-old seeks to discover himself is through dramatic play where he takes the role of characters about whom he has read or whom he has seen or heard. While the six-year-old's imitations are veridical, the eight-year-old's imitations are truly dramatic in that the child really tries to play the part, although it is often for a comic effect. Coupled with these attempts to discover himself and others through role playing is an increased self-consciousness and sensitivity to his differences from other people. At about third grade children start to feel the impact of social status, clothing, and appearance differences, which begin to count in his self-evaluation. The extent to which they count and affect the child's self-concept will vary with the circumstances of his life and those of his classmates.

In his social relations, the eight-year-old is usually friendly and cooperative. He is less persistent in his activities at home and not as helpful around the house as he was at age seven. His helpfulness is now more closely associated with his momentary mood than with a desire to help. Perhaps because of his new maturity and self-awareness, the eight-year-old wants mature jobs around the house, such as fixing things or cooking and baking, that are adult-like activities. When the eight-year-old is asked to do what he regards as "baby" jobs, such as picking up things or even setting the table, he may grumble because he thinks such chores are beneath him.

Because of his new concern with his self, the eight-year-old is particularly concerned with how his mother and father think and feel about him. He may often dog their footsteps and hang upon every word and facial expression, hoping for clues of their reaction to him. The eight-year-old is also discovering that parents are not perfect and can make mistakes. His attitude towards his parents is thus complex and ambivalent—a combination of love, demandingness, anger, and criticalness. Just as he tries himself out on others, the eight-year-old tries out his parents by confronting them with a multitude of burdensome demands: "Do this" or "make this," and so on.

Relations of the eight-year-old with his younger brothers and sisters will again vary with the size of the family and the age separation of the children. In general, however, the eight-year-old is less maternal and paternal in his attitude than was true at age seven. In contrast to this backsliding in sibling relationships is the eight-year-old's relationship to his friends. Seeing and being with friends is now one of the dominant motives in going to school. Friendships between children at this age tend to be closer and more exacting than heretofore. The basis of the relationship is beginning to shift from the engagement in common play activities to some of the personality characteristics of the children involved. "Sarah is bossy" or "Harold always wants to fight" reflects a new sensitivity to the nature of the friendship relationship and a reduced concern with the shared activity itself.

With regard to adults, the eight-year-old is often more polite with strangers than he is at home. He has learned the basic social routines of greeting and giving and taking and uses "thank you" and "please" appropriately and without prompting. The quality of his interaction with adults is now more mature and he talks "with" them rather than "to" them. On the phone, for example, the eight-year-old will take a message and even ask questions if something is not clear. He likes to meet new people and to go to new places and looks forward to family vacations away from home.

At age eight, children generally enjoy and look forward to school, although the reasons, as already noted, are less academic than they are social. The presence of bosom friends makes school attractive to this age group. Attendance is usually very good indeed, and when a child is absent he wants to make up what he has missed and catch up on what has been happening with his friends while he was gone. Like the six-year-old, the child of eight is once again interested in taking things home, perhaps again to see mother's reaction. He spontaneously talks about what he did in school so that his parents learn more about what he did in school than they ever learned before.

The relationship with the teacher is also different from that at age seven. He is less concerned with the teacher and is more concerned with the group. Although he works independently, he still needs to have directions read and reread to him. Eight-year-old children may gossip more among themselves and begin sending notes to one another. Sometimes these interruptions get out of hand and a child has to be disciplined. Such discipline often involves separating him from the group and seating him close to the teacher. In the attempt to discipline the eight-year-old child, it is necessary to recognize his new-found sociability and the prominence that it currently has in his life. The manifestation of a growth process should not be mistaken for perversity or lack of good upbringing.

It was mentioned earlier that the eight-year-old is judgmental, and this holds true for his own schoolwork, which he is constantly evaluating. He mentioned the number of mistakes ("I got four wrong") and criticizes his own artwork. Indeed many children who were avid artists at the age of six or seven begin to give up art by age eight or nine because they come to recognize the discrepancy between what they have been trying to render and what they have actually drawn. Their discouragement in this regard is often carried over into adulthood. Most grown-ups say they can't draw. The eight-year-old is critical of himself in other respects and is very sensitive about being a slow reader or about being poor in spelling. Because the child's academic standing is known by all children in the classroom, it often determines their behavior towards him. The child who is teased or snickered at must defend himself, but he also builds into his self-concept many negative ideas because of the way in which peers treat him.

This, in brief, is the eight-year-old. He is outgoing, curious, and extremely social. He is judgmental and critical both of himself and others and is demanding in his efforts to get more information about himself. He is more mature in social relations and talks with, rather than to, adults. Friends are extremely important at this age and become the prime reason for his interest in school and for his good attendance. His ambivalence about growing up is shown in his criticalness of adults, on the one hand, and, on the other, in his eagerness to know more about the adult world and to assume some of its prerogatives.

The Nine-Year-Old

There is no sharp separation between the characteristics of the eight- and the nine-year-old but rather an increase in the maturity and refinement of behaviors exhibited earlier. The eight-year-old's judgmental tendencies are continued by the nine-year-old with greater objectivity and discernment. The nine-year-old can say "That's not so hot, is it?" of something she has done and not feel anxious or guilty about it. In a like manner the nine-year-old will appraise parents and other adults calmly and dispassionately. The initial shock of discovering that parents are not perfect is long since past, and the nine-year-old can accept parental mistakes and ignorance as a matter of course.

This does not in any way mean that the nine-year-old is an automated robot with no feelings. She still shows the bursts of emotion and impatience characteristic of children, but the outbursts are less frequent and are under greater self-control. In addition, while the eight-year-old was pushed and pulled by other events, the nine-year-old seems to have found her own inner gyroscope, which directs her into particular activities of her own choosing in which she can become deeply involved. While working on a stamp collection or building a model, she can become so absorbed that she entirely forgets time and meals. If she is forced to interrupt her activity she comes back to it on her own.

Perhaps because of this inner-directed quality of her behavior, the nine-year-old appears to be more of a "solid citizen" than she was at eight. She gives the impression of calm, steadfastness, and responsibility that will be the benchmarks of her later maturity. This new maturity is seen in her dealings with adults and peers, wherein she exhibits a depth of consideration and a sense of fairness beyond what she was capable of at age eight. Just as she can accept her own failures and mistakes with greater equanimity, she is better able to accept blame and responsibility for her actions. She is at the point now where she distinguishes between the damage done by the act and the intentions that led to it and gives intentions more weight than damage in judgments.

There is also at age nine an increased awareness of sex and sex-appropriate behaviors. Girls at this stage may become upset and angry about their clothing and appearance. Some girls may even throw tantrums, saying, "I hate the way I look" or "I hate this dress." Nine-year-old girls may begin to give parents a hard time about clothes if they believe what they have is not expensive or fashionable enough. In sharp contrast, and perhaps to accentuate their masculinity, boys are disdainful of their clothes and of cleanliness, so that parents must constantly urge them to wash with soap and to change underwear and socks. These sex-stereotyped behaviors are culturally conditioned and are changing as society becomes less rigid about "sex-appropriate" behaviors.

If we look now at the self-concept of the nine-year-old, we observe a new self-confidence that derives from her having herself better under control and being better able to resist external pressures towards activity. Perhaps this heightened self-confidence also comes from her new tendency to organize and budget her time (often with the aid of lists and schedules), which gives her a new sense of self-importance. Time must indeed be budgeted, for the middle-class child is now attending church functions and Scout meetings and taking lessons of one sort or another, as well as being involved in organized peer-group activities. Parents of nine-year-old youngsters often begin to feel more like chauffeurs or cabdrivers than parents.

It is in the context of this heightened self-confidence that the nine-year-old child's self-derogatory remarks must be taken. In a healthy personality, self-derogation is a sign of emotional security and self-assurance. It takes a certain robustness of self-concept to proclaim "I was wrong," and the nine-year-old apparently has this robustness. She can admit her own negative qualities and express her wish that she were different without feeling guilty or anxious about these admissions.

The new maturity and self-confidence of age nine can be seen in her relations to parents. There is less quarreling, and she is much less demanding of parental attention. The intense period of testing out adult reactions is over and gives place in the nine-year-old to self-motivated absorption in many different activities. One can observe the nine-year-old's new maturity in still another way. She does not need to be bribed or bargained with to do simple chores and will accept them as her responsibility and contribution to the family. She may, however, have to be reminded about what she was supposed to do.

In general, the nine-year-old's relations with her mother and father are friendly and accommodating. While she enjoys outings and doings with her father and mother, her own friends and activities absorb her so that she does not make demands upon her parents, as she once did, to alleviate her boredom. In a like manner, the nine-year-old generally gets along well with her younger brothers and sisters but may be a nuisance to her teenage siblings.

The close friendships with peers begun at age eight are continued and strengthened at age nine. Such friendships are strictly between youngsters of the same sex, and there is much overt verbal hostility between boys and girls. Boys are said by girls to be "always fighting and yelling," while boys complain that girls are always "laughing and giggling." At this age organized games with rules, such as baseball, football, and basketball, are becoming more common among the boys,* and both girls and boys may begin to form clubs about various activities. Again, the friendships and companionship of the peer group become a powerful motivating force for liking school and for good school attendance.

School in general is easier for age nine. She no longer has trouble getting started in the morning, although she may forget to take her homework or books. In some respects the nine-year-old is hard on her teacher because she now knows what she wants to do and what she does not want to do and does not hesitate to say so. Materials and information are now what attract the nine-year-old, who is emotionally less attached to her teacher than she was heretofore. Now her dislike for a subject can generalize to a dislike of the teacher rather than the reverse. Moreover, her wish for independence in pursuing a subject may lead her to neglect getting help when she really needs it.

Academic achievement is of considerable importance to the nine-year-old, perhaps because it is a prime standard of evaluation used by children in ranking one another. It is, however, usually the children at the extremes who suffer the most. The slow child relative to her peers is usually singled out and grouped separately, and everyone knows who is in the "slow" group. In contrast, the very bright children are sometimes regarded as strange or as teacher's pets and are often shunned to the same extent as the slow child. The ideal seems to be the child who gets good, but not perfect, grades without expending too much effort. Many children who could do better often conform to this middle-of-the-road ideal for social reasons.

By the age of nine the mechanics of reading and arithmetic have been mastered, and these skills can now be used for gaining information, for solving problems, and for games and recreation. Writing may still be sloppy at age nine, and children of this age may complain about having a poor memory. Nine-year-olds also take their tool skills outside the classroom, read books on their own, and use their arithmetic in their purchases at the store. At this age, children begin to discover some of the fringe benefits of literacy.

---

*This situation is changing slowly as girls are being encouraged to participate in team sports. Some of the aggressiveness of boys and their "groupiness" may be attributed to their participation in team sports. Girls can be expected to behave in a similar manner as their participation in team sports increases.

The nine-year-old, then, shows a new maturity, self-confidence, and independence from adults. She is inner-directed and self-motivated. Her friendships are more solid, but her separation from the opposite sex is greater than it was at age eight. The skills learned in school are at last being put to practical use outside the classroom, which enhances their value and significance and furthers the child's interest in learning. While her independence can at times be trying, it is often easier on adults than the demandingness of younger children.

The Ten-Year-Old

At the end of his first decade of life, the young person reaches a high point of balance and adaptation to his world that he may not achieve again for another decade. By the age of ten he has crossed and recrossed the stormy seas of home, school, and immediate community so that he is a seasoned traveler in these domains. Because they no longer hold terrors or difficulties for him, he enjoys them and takes pride in his ability to "fit in" at home, at school, and at play with his peers. Because he has mastered the trials and tribulations of childhood and because the new conflicts and frustrations of adolescence are still far away, the ten year-old is at peace with himself and his world. It is, relatively speaking, a halcyon period in human development.

There are, to be sure, some exceptions to the general picture of solid adaptation presented by the ten-year-old. He does, on occasion, get extremely angry, depressed, or sad. Such moments are, however, usually short-lived and quickly forgotten. Other negative aspects of "ten-year-oldness" are equally minor in nature. There is still little concern, particularly on the part of boys, for clothes, which are given very rough treatment and which are often left scattered about. In contrast, most ten-year-old children are pretty good about not losing their belongings.

At ten, girls are slightly more advanced sexually than boys and already give evidence of that rapid sprint to maturity that in the next couple of years will make them taller and heavier than boys of the same age. Girls are already beginning to manifest in their bodies the rounding and softening of contours that will continue into adolescence. Some ten-year-old girls may even experience increased rounding in the breast area, together with a tightening and protrusion of the nipples. Concern about their bodies, about menstruation, and about sexual activity in general is beginning to appear in girls. Among boys, in whom physical changes are less marked, concern with the body and with approaching physical maturity is much less noticeable.

Aside from these concerns about approaching maturity, much more prevalent among girls than among boys, ten-year-olds are remarkably stable youngsters. Fears and anxieties are at an all-time low, whereas relations with parents, with teachers, and with peers are at an all-time high. The exception is relations with younger siblings between the ages of six and nine, who, perhaps because they remind ten of what he himself just went through in the way of adaptive struggles, are not treated well by the ten-year-old.

If we look more closely at the self-concept at age ten, the changes from age nine are worth mention. At nine, the child was self-conscious and somewhat self-critical, although accepting of this criticism. By ten, however, the young person shows much less interest in evaluating himself and seems to accept himself as he is without worrying too much about his strengths and weaknesses. He experiences a general feeling of well-being — a feeling that ten is just the right age, not too little and not too big. He has enough but not too much responsibility and freedom. To be sure, he looks forward to growing up, marrying, and having a career, and his ideal models are either parents, or famous people such as motion picture stars or popular athletes. Growing up is still a very romantic idea, and ten years old is a romantic age.

In general then, the ten-year-old is self-accepting. He likes his body and his looks, he likes what he can do in the way of sport — which is considerable — and what he can do academically. His own self-acceptance is heightened by the acceptance accorded him by peers, by family, and by the school. There is a sort of mutual admiration society between the ten-year-old and his social world, which supports and reinforces his positive self-image, his self-confidence, and his self-acceptance.

At age ten, the youngster really likes his family and thinks that it is the greatest. He enjoys going on family trips and outings, and does not resent spending the time with family rather than with friends. The ten-year-old discovers a new liking and respect for his parents, whose concerns about his eating and dress are now regarded as genuine expressions of concern and are appreciated even if they are not heeded. Both boys and girls go out of their way to be helpful and are spontaneous in their show of affection and concern. Children discover new qualities to value in their parents, particularly as companions or competitors in sports and games. The ten-year-old child is, in a very real sense, a family person.

Outside the home, interpersonal relations are equally good, and the ten-year-old likes and enjoys his friends. Sex differences in friendship patterns are also beginning to emerge. Boys are already beginning to move in loosely organized groups of boys who may play basketball, football, or baseball together. Within the group boys may have particular friends, but there is a lot of switching around. Girls usually move in smaller groups and are likely to form more intense friendships and have more serious "fallings out" with the girls, being "mad" and "not playing" or "not speaking" to one another as a consequence. Much of this is, of course, sex-stereotyped behavior that is changing as girls participate in more traditionally "male" activities.

Age ten is a good one for organized group activities, and it is one of the most enthusiastic ages for such organizations as Scouts and Little League. Indeed, ten-year-olds often form groups of their own, which may have secret meeting places, codes, passwords, and insignia. Such clubs may also have high moral standards regarding such things as secrecy and helping others. However, the groups are often short-lived because they belong to the romantic fantasy or whim of the moment and do not meet some deep need for companionship upon which lasting group organizations are built. The ten-year-old's good relationship with his family almost precludes any lasting commitment to a fixed peer group.

The good adjustment of the ten-year-old can also be seen in his school behavior. By and large, he likes school and is a responsible student. He accepts his assignments and gets them done without getting sidetracked and without having to rush to get them done in time. The ten-year-old likes his teacher and accepts his or her authority and knowledge. He may even quote him or her at home and describe the teacher's physical appearance to parents. Teachers are liked if they are fair and not partial to particular students and if they are firm but not strict. At age ten, children like the teacher to schedule activities and like to keep to the schedule.

Children of this age still enjoy being read to by their teachers and enjoy books such as *Robinson Crusoe* or *Treasure Island*. Mystery and adventure stories are in very great demand at this age by both girls and boys. Girls seem to prefer, however, that the hero be feminine, as in the Nancy Drew stories. At this age, too, girls are beginning to show the interest in animals, particularly horses, that is so widespread among girls in pre- and early adolescence and that persists in many women throughout life. Boys, on the other hand, do not as yet show the interest in automobiles that will be their guiding concern as they move into adolescence. TV watching is still frequent, but the ten-year-old is more selective than at earlier ages.

In his studying and academic pursuits, the ten-year-old lacks some of the stick-to-itiveness of the nine-year-old. Prolonged periods of activity have to be interrupted by getting up and moving about. At ten the young person is also somewhat more superficial and is more interested in learning facts and memorizing names than he is in finding causes and explanations. Even his interest in mystery and adventure is more closely tied to the excitement—the what-comes-next aspect—than it is to the logic of the crime or mystery. Within the school setting, then, the ten-year-old prefers to soak up information rather than to integrate or to digest it. And perhaps this is a necessary preparation for the attempts at integration that will come later.

In summary, the ten-year-old is at the high point of childhood. He is well adapted to his body, family, friends, and school. These no longer hold any mystery or fears for him, and he likes people and likes himself. Although there are occasional emotional outbursts and continued rough treatment of clothes, the ten-year-old is a joy to have about the house or in the classroom. He is cooperative, considerate, and responsible to authority. Looking ahead, we know that the halcyon days of the ten-year-old are the calm before the storm and that nature, perhaps in her wisdom, perhaps in her spite, conceals all the signs of storm and stress that will arise in adolescence.

The Eleven-Year-Old

In some respects the age of ten is a kind of plateau between childhood and adolescence. At age ten the child can look at where she has been without regressing and to where she is going without beginning the climb. As she moves towards the age of eleven, however, the growth pressures reassert themselves, and the accelerated pace of growth that marks early adolescence can be seen and felt. The halcyon period for parents and siblings is over, as it is for teachers and other adults who have to deal with young people. There is no growth without conflict, and the eleven-year-old is entering a new phase of growth and hence renewed conflicts.

The new growth thrust of the eleven-year-old is revealed in numerous ways. For one thing, her activity level shows a marked increase, and she has trouble keeping still. In this respect she is reminiscent of the six-year-old. Her appetite, too, seems to have increased severalfold, and her stomach, to parents at least, seems like a bottomless pit. It is not only her appetite for food that is voracious; so too is her appetite for new experience, for knowledge about the world, and, most particularly, for more information about people.

Perhaps because of her tremendous energy and activity, she often forgets her manners and is loud, boorish, and rude. In stores or on the bus, the eleven-year-old will shout loudly at her friends and push towards them without sufficient consideration for the people in her way. On her bike or skateboard she may take chances in traffic that cause drivers to slam on their brakes and shake their heads. Perhaps the eleven-year-old, sensing that she is closer to adulthood than to childhood, wants to defy that adult world one last time under the aegis of childhood.

Her defiance of adult authority comes out in other ways as well. Quarreling is a common feature of eleven-year-old behavior, but she likes to do the arguing and doesn't like to be argued at by others. Not only is she argumentative, she is also rather emotional and subject to outbursts of rage, peevishness, and moodiness. The emotional control of the ten-year-old seems to have vanished by age eleven, when the young person is often touchy and unpredictable. In part, this new emotionality is due to the increased pace of growth and the concomitant recognition that she is growing up. This awareness of an impending change in status brings both hope and new anxieties and fears that make for the special sensitivity of this period.

Often the sensitivity, emotionality, and argumentativeness is more in evidence at home than outside the home. Particularly with strangers, the eleven-year-old can be cooperative, friendly, lively, and pleasant. On a short-term basis she can be quite easy to take, and it is only under prolonged relations that her negative features begin to manifest themselves. The eleven-year-old needs to be handled with understanding but with firmness. Although she cannot be allowed to ride rough-shod over people, she should not be put down too harshly.

When we look more closely at the eleven-year-old's self-concept and the reactions of others towards her, she hardly appears to be the same person she was a year earlier. Because of her new press towards activity and her consequent carelessness, she is often yelled at and disciplined. This in turn results in a belligerent attitude to the effect that "everything I do is wrong" and "you are always picking on me." The calm self-confidence of the ten-year-old has given way to renewed doubt and sensitivity about herself. Perhaps nothing could better illustrate how much the self-concept is dependent upon others' reactions than the rapid transformation that comes about between the ages of ten and eleven in general self-confidence.

As she feels herself moving towards a new level of maturity, she makes a new search for self-definition. Such definition, we know, comes through confrontation with others, and the eleven-year-old often confronts adults, particularly parents, with criticism and accusations as if to get a response—any kind of response. Eleven needs to be noticed and cannot tolerate indifference. Even negative reactions from parents are better than nothing, and eleven often lashes out without really understanding why she attacks as she does. Coupled with this new sensitivity and desire to be noticed is a new defensiveness. While she will admit faults, she will do so only in a general way and will not be pinned down to specifics.

The independence from parental influence that will become progressively greater during the next few years begins at age eleven. At this age boys and girls are beginning to differ with their parents as to what profession or career to choose and are beginning to make their own choices. Perhaps as a result of the new attacks on their self-confidence and acceptance, many eleven-year-olds compensate with dreams of being at the center of the stage as singers, actors, musicians, or famous authors. In a phrase, the eleven-year-old often dreams of being famous.

Both boys and girls engage in fantasies about the future. These are concerned with their future professions, and young people are often highly specific in their choices. But they also engage in thinking about marriage and some of the qualities they would like to have in their future mates. They say, although their behavior belies this, that they are more interested in

personality characteristics such as kindness, understanding, and
honesty than they are in good looks. They want their prospec-
tive partners to be reasonably intelligent and nice-looking and
people with whom they can communicate.

The changed self-concept of the eleven-year-old accom-
panies a radical change in the character of her interpersonal
relationships. Whereas at age ten, the young person accepted
parental authority, she now challenges it. She is critical of her
mother's judgment and of her father's temper. Child-rearing
practices in the home are challenged, and parents' motives and
feelings become the subject of the eleven-year-old's attacks,
particularly if she feels that favoritism has been shown to
younger siblings. While there may be periods of respite when the
eleven-year-old will get along well with parents, it is hard to
know when the next negative mood will strike.

Friendships with peers do not suffer the same revolution
that is true for the eleven-year-old's relations with her parents.
The choice of friendships is now made on the basis of mutuality
of interest and temperament rather than on the basis of proximity and common activity, as heretofore. At this age boys usually
have one best friend and a group of other friends who play
together. Girls, in contrast, tend to be part of a small group of
friends, all of whom are good friends and among whom pairing
is less frequent.

Relations between boys and girls also change, and
eleven-year-olds, both boys and girls, will admit that they are
interested in the opposite sex or soon will be. Girls are likely to
be more interested and more vocal about their interest than are
boys. They talk about boys a good deal of the time and describe
boys in what is often excruciating detail. Boys show their interest in girls by the joking, teasing, and "showing off" in front of
them that is so common at this stage. Girls, in turn, begin to
enjoy this behavior because they recognize it as an expression of
positive interest and a primitive effort to gain attention and to
be attractive.

The changes at eleven that appear in other spheres of life
also appear in the school setting. While many eleven-year-old
youngsters continue to like school, many others find that school
has now become a problem for them. And, it must be added,
they are often a problem for the school. The eleven-year-old's
high energy level and criticalness make it difficult for her to sit
still and to finish her work at a single sitting and without disturbing others. School is enjoyed mostly because it is where the

eleven-year-old's friends are, and young people at this age would like to spend most of their time gossiping with their friends.

Eleven-year-old children do not dislike school but rather are very specific in what they do and do not want to learn. Perhaps because of the pressure for activity, the eleven-year-old doesn't like material that is complex and prefers material that can be learned easily and can be used competitively. At this age the young person delights in showing her skill in rote abilities such as spelling, multiplication, and addition. But she has trouble understanding relations and more complex combinations of events. It is not that she is stupid but only that her energies are directed in so many ways that she does not have enough to expend on academic concentration. Learning often fatigues her because she is spending her energies so lavishly elsewhere.

At age eleven then, we begin to see the changes that will mark adolescence. The pace of growth is beginning to accelerate and there is an increase in energy and activity level. Self-doubts and insecurity are once again present and there is a new defensiveness apparent in the young person's reluctance to admit her weaknesses. Relations to parents and siblings are once again conflictual, and the eleven-year-old finds much to criticize in her parents. She believes that she is being put upon and discriminated against. Only her relations with her friends remain unruffled. At school, there is a new dislike, or at least impatience, of school and school subjects. At this age young people are more interested in materials that can be memorized or learned by formula than materials that require reasoning and problem solving. This attitude towards school may simply reflect the fact that at this stage young people do not have the energy to invest in concentrated learning; they expend it too generously elsewhere.

In closing this chapter on the unique characteristics of each age level, it is perhaps well to emphasize again that these are ideal descriptions. No single child will conform in all respects to the pictures outlined here. These descriptions are provided as general guides and to illustrate the cyclical and upward thrust of growth with its periods of inwardness and quiet and of outwardness and activity. The aim of the descriptions is thus mainly to acquaint the reader with the processes of growth as they appear in children so that the manifestations of these processes will not be mistaken for personal quirks or emotional problems.

PART III

The Adolescent

9 Personal and Social Development

Early adolescence, roughly the years from twelve to sixteen, is an allegro of rapid growth that propels the child toward adulthood. It is the period in which the young person attains adult stature and appearance. By the time the adolescent is sixteen she has attained sexual maturity, in the physical sense at any rate, and is capable of procreation. Finally, during the years from twelve to sixteen the adolescent develops formal or abstract thinking abilities that permit her to engage in scientific and philosophical thinking, to plan realistically for the future, and to understand the historical past.

These changes, and many more that occur during early adolescence, do not transform the young person into an entirely different individual. The social patterns that were solidified during childhood are carried forward into adolescence. The social leader in elementary school often becomes the social leader in junior high school, and the athletic child often becomes a football, basketball, or baseball player in junior and senior high school. In the same way, the scholarly child often maintains her pattern in the secondary school. Marked changes in social style can and do occur, of course, but continuity remains the rule rather than the exception.

The continuity between childhood and adolescence is maintained in more than the persistence of certain physical and personality features. Many of the interpersonal problems and issues that the child confronts are again met by the adolescent, although in somewhat different form. These problems and issues between parents and children are at once intellectual and emotional. We can look at these issues in the context of parent-child contracts regarding responsibility-freedom, achievement-support, and loyalty-commitment, which we discussed in Chapter 6.

Part 2, "The Adolescent" is from Parish Planning for Grades 7–10, edited by James Simpson. The Board of Christian Education of the United Presbyterian Church in the United States of America. Copyright © 1969. Used by permission.

In adolescence, for example, the young person demands freedoms that she never even thought of as a child. She wishes to take the car on a weekend trip, or take flying lessons, or take a trip with her friends. Parents, on their side, demand new responsibilities. They assume that the adolescent will take care of clothing and personal hygiene without having to be constantly reminded. Furthermore, parents demand that adolescents take responsibility in the area of sexual behavior, in the matter of late hours, and in the use of alcohol, tobacco, and other drugs. The freedoms demanded by adolescents and the responsibilities asked by their parents are thus quite different in kind from the freedoms demanded by the child (say, to stay up late) and the responsibilities required by parents of the child (to be cautious when riding a bicycle in the street).

We see a similar transformation in the contract having to do with achievement and support. Adolescents, like children, want intellectual, emotional, and material support from their parents but want it given in a different way than it was in childhood. The adolescent doesn't usually want parents to show affection by kissing and fondling but rather by a sympathetic attitude towards her problems and a tolerance of her mood swings and occasional backslides towards childlike pursuits and interests. Likewise, while parents continue to want their children to get good grades, do well in sports, and be socially popular, the demand is somewhat different than it was in childhood. Whereas in childhood social popularity consisted in playing well with other children, in adolescence it includes elements of physical attractiveness, personality, and social skill, which are less under the adolescent's personal control. For some adolescents, it may be more difficult to meet parental expectations regarding such things as social popularity than it was during childhood.

Finally, there are equally prominent changes in the contract having to do with loyalty and commitment. During the elementary school years the child asks only that her parents be committed to her in the sense of devoting time to her, her interests, and her achievements. In adolescence, however, the young person is not so concerned about having time with parents as she is with the parents' commitment to the values they espouse and to future generations. Parents, on their part, also change their demands. During childhood they expect their children to place parents above all other people in their affections. In adolescence, this is no longer possible, and parents demand instead loyalty to the values and beliefs (religious, political, etc.) to which they are committed.

It is clear, then, that while adolescence is a period of transformation from childhood to adulthood, it is a continuous rather than a discontinuous process. Not only do physical, personality, and characterological traits persist from childhood through adulthood, but also the problems and conflicts that the adolescent encounters in her two steps forward, one step backward, march to adulthood are similar to issues and conflicts she encountered as a child and will meet again as an adult. In particular, the parent-child contracts of freedom-responsibility, achievement-support, and loyalty-commitment are maintained despite significant changes in content. Without discounting, then, the very real metamorphosis that adolescence brings about, one should not overlook the prominent continuities from childhood to adulthood.

Facets of Growth and Development

Physical Development

Physical growth from birth to adolescence, while continuous, frequently changes its pace. Growth during the first year of life is very rapid, and the infant usually grows about 8 inches in height and triples his birth weight. The rate of growth declines gradually thereafter until adolescence, when there is again a period of rapid growth in height and weight. In general, the greatest increment in standing height for girls occurs at around the age of eleven, with an average increase of about 2.5 inches. For boys, the period of most rapid growth in height is, on the average, the thirteenth year, with increments from 4 to 6 inches. Weight, on the other hand, tends to increase rather regularly through adolescence, although in mid-adolescence it frequently drops for girls. In this connection it is well to recall that the average thirteen-year-old girl is both taller and heavier than the average thirteen-year-old boy.

Equally dramatic as the sudden growth of height in adolescence is the onset of puberty or sexual maturity. Although the age range across which puberty can occur for girls is as much as ten years, over 75 percent have their first menstrual period at twelve, thirteen, or fourteen years. However, the fact that a girl begins to menstruate does not mean necessarily that she is fertile and can conceive a child. Fertility depends upon a complex of factors in which ovulation is a necessary but not sufficient condition. Other bodily changes associated with puberty in girls tend to occur, on the average, in the following order: breast development, 10.7 years; pubic hair, 11.5 years; axillary (underarm) hair, 12.5 years; menarche (menstruation), 13.1 years. In other words, many secondary sex characteristics appear before the first menstrual period.

It is much more difficult to determine the exact date of puberty in males, but in terms of such indices as ejaculation, voice change, nocturnal emissions, and pubic hair, the age of thirteen is modal, the age below which half the boys have attained these traits and above which the other half attain them. In general, then, boys appear to reach sexual maturity, on the average, about two years after girls do. As with girls, there are wide individual differences, and some boys may attain puberty at the age of ten, while others may not attain it until age sixteen.

The age at which puberty appears is determined by many different factors. Some recent studies suggest that the age of menarche for girls has decreased dramatically during the last hundred years for developed countries. In contrast to the age of thirteen, the average for girls in America today, the usual age for first menstruation was seventeen a hundred years ago. Hereditary and nutritional factors appear to play an important role, and undernourished children may be retarded in the age at which they attain puberty. The most recent data on physical growth suggest that American adolescents are no longer getting taller or attaining menarche at an earlier age than previous generations did. Apparently we have reached our biological limits in these regards.

An important aspect of physical growth in adolescence, because it has to do with that all-important question of appearance, is the changes that occur in the facial bones and features. In general, bones increase in density, hardness, and size in the course of development, and this can lead to quite radical changes in physical appearance. During adolescence, the nose and mouth widen, the nose becomes longer and more prominent, and the jaw juts out farther. Generally the top part of the face grows more rapidly than the lower part, so the chin is about the last feature to attain its adult configuration. This may come as some consolation to fourteen-year-olds whose faces seem a little nose-heavy because the lower part of the face has not yet caught up with the growth of nose and forehead.

Other physical changes occur as well. Increases in strength, for example, are related to extent of sexual development. Body hair darkens and lengthens for both boys and girls. In addition, certain types of sweat glands, inoperative in childhood, begin to secrete a fatty substance in adolescence that gives rise to the well-publicized body odor. Changes in the distribution of fat over the body and in the size and capacity of the respiratory and digestive systems also occur during adolescence.

It needs to be emphasized that there are very wide individual differences in the rate of physical development during puberty. We have already noted that such variations are related to culture, nutrition, and heredity. Early or late maturing is often a family trait and is related to body build. Young people with relatively squat, heavy builds are likely to attain puberty earlier than young people with tall, slender figures. Young people with average body configuations are likely to attain puberty at the ages described above.

Early and late maturity has different consequences for boys and girls. Late maturing is less of a handicap for a girl, whose parents are perfectly happy that boys' interest in her is delayed, as is her interest in them. She also misses that period of being out of step (in the sense of being taller and heavier) with boys her own age. She can maintain rapport with boys her own age as well as with girls who have reached puberty but who wish not to emphasize it. The early maturing girl is, however, somewhat handicapped. She is more mature than both boys and girls her age and is subjected to social experiences, such as the glances of men and boys, for which she may not be prepared. Because she *appears* older than her actual age, she may be expected to *be* older in her behavior, and that is also a burden added to the fact that she must look to older adolescents for friendship. Although she is looked up to by more slowly maturing girls, this does not fully compensate for some of the social pressures she experiences.

The situation is just the reverse for boys. The early maturing boy is generally admired by his peers for his greater strength, athletic ability, and general prowess. Although he too may be

expected to take on responsibilities that are too advanced for
him, this is softened by his ability to maintain friendships among his own age group, particularly the girls, who welcome boys their age who are at least equally mature. Slow-maturing boys have a more difficult time. Such boys usually keep their baby fat, rosy cheeks, and high voices, so they are frequently the butts of teasing and jokes. Their lack of strength and coordination keeps them from being active participants in the sports and other activities of their peers. They often take jobs such as "manager" of a team in order to participate, if in an indirect way, in athletic events. Early or late maturation in adolescence can, then, present some very real personality problems for some young people.

Sexual Development

The advent of puberty brings about new feelings, new interests, new attitudes, and many new problems that are, in large measure, different for girls and boys. While boy-girl differences are present from the start of life, it is only at adolescence that sexual status supersedes age status. A child is always a child first and a boy or a girl second, but in adolescence the young person is a boy or girl first and an adolescent second. Put differently, while it is reasonable to generalize about children without regard to sex, that is hazardous when we talk about adolescents.

Although the physiological maturity of girls is clearly evidenced by the menarche, there is no concomitant immediate increase in sexual desire. In general, the girl's sexuality is much more general and much less focused than is the boy's. She is not as easily aroused as the boy and is aroused by different sorts of stimuli. Whereas boys are aroused by nudity and actions that are suggestive of disrobement, girls are more stimulated by "sweet talk" and tenderness, on the one hand, and by excitement and danger, on the other hand. These differences may, in part at least, be culturally conditioned. The current popularity of magazines for women featuring male centerfolds is but one indication that females as well as males can be stimulated by nudity.

The girl's interest in boys is generally earlier than the boy's interest in girls. Girls' "boy consciousness" often takes the form of wanting to be noticed and admired by a particular boy.

There is, at the same time, much concentrated and animated discussion among girls about boys. As in other areas, however, interest in boys and in dating varies widely among individual girls. Some girls get into the social swim at an early age, while others are content to wait until they are in senior high or beyond before they begin to date.

In addition to producing new experiences, interests, and attitudes, sexual maturity brings new problems. Girls who suddenly fill out must learn to deal with the new attention that is paid to them by boys and men and must learn to cope with the whistles and the long head-to-toe appraisals given them as they walk by on the street. In addition, they must learn to cope with boys on intimate terms. While the girl finds kissing and petting pleasurable and feels no pressure to go further, this is not true for the boy, who feels that climactic release is the only purpose of the foreplay. When the girls stops, the boy feels cheated, and the girl cannot understand how the sweet boy she was so tenderly stroking became such a panting, aggressive monster. As has often been said, the boy is erotic while the girl is romantic.

Again, these differences have probably been exaggerated by sex-role stereotyping. Many women today are willing to admit their erotic needs, and many men are willing to acknowledge their romantic tendencies. In the end, it may be that the erotic/romantic distinction is not so much a dichotomy *between* sexes as a dichotomy *within* each sex.

Once her femininity is clearly established, the girl still must establish her sense of sexual identity. This is a complicated part of her whole self-conception and involves her ideas about her attractiveness, her capacity to produce and raise children, and her unique abilities and talents as a person. The attainment of sexual identity for girls is more difficult today, when women are offered equality in some regards and not in others and when new career opportunities are becoming available. The reconciliation of the wife-mother concept of female identity with the career woman concept of personal identity is a very real problem for many young women today.

The advent of puberty occasions new experiences, attitudes, and problems for boys as well as girls. The boy finds that he is suddenly interested in looking at girls, particularly at those who have large attractions. He finds that he has spontaneous erections and becomes concerned that they will be noticed. While he and most of his friends engage in secret and solitary masturbation, there is much overt joking and denial of this activity in locker rooms and playgrounds. Masturbation is more common among middle-class boys than it is among boys from the lower-class, where direct outlets for sexual tension are more socially sanctioned than they are among middle-class youth.

While girls are interested in boys even during childhood, although they may conceal it, boys' interest in girls really emerges only during the thirteenth or fourteenth year. Again, the boys' interest in girls is somewhat different from the girls' interest in boys. Girls are seen, fantasied, and talked about as objects of sexual relations rather than as persons or future mates. Studies, for example, suggest that boys (and even men) judge women first upon their attractiveness and only secondarily upon personality, whereas the reverse holds true for girls and women.

As boys and girls attend parties together, go to dances, and date they become familiar with certain patterns and codes to be followed. Petting, for example, is rigidly codified among adolescents. Young people thus become increasingly more comfortable with the opposite sex and, towards the end of adolescence, are frequently found more in the company of the opposite sex than of the same sex. Relationships become more mature as well and the older adolescent boy begins to take an interest in the kind of girl he dates as well as her attractiveness. Girls, on their side, increasingly evaluate the boys whom they date in terms of the sort of husband and father they would make.

Psychological Developments

From the psychological point of view, the major task of adolescence is the establishment of a stable and resilient personal identity. We now know that a sense of personal identity is not inherent in being born a discrete organism; it is a product of integrative effort. One aspect of growing up is that the young person learns a great deal about himself, not all of which is good or compatible with other aspects of himself. He learns that he is attractive or unattractive, calm or peppery, passive or aggressive, well coordinated or clumsy, and so on. He also learns that he must behave one way towards parents, another way towards peers and siblings, and still other ways towards relatives, teachers and friends. He discovers that these various people, in turn, treat him differently than he is treated by his parents and hold different opinions about him. These are but some of the kinds of data the child collects about himself.

During adolescence his task is to bring all of this knowledge about himself together and to arrange it into some meaningful, workable whole that he can call himself and with which he can live reasonably well. In a sense, then, the personal identity that the adolescent must construct is built out of a host of separate identities: sexual, familial, racial, religious, ethnic, peer, student, and so on. It is only during adolescence that, for the first time, the young person becomes aware of how many different roles he plays. His job is to integrate these into a sense of "they are all me."

One way in which the work on identity formation goes on is through attempts to adopt the identities of famous or admired persons. Adolescent boys will copy the voice qualities and body swagger of certain movie heroes, and girls may copy the hair styles and movements of certain admired screen goddesses. Work on identity formation also goes on during those "lazy" periods during which adolescents are apparently doing nothing but lying on their backs listening to records for hours on end. Identity formation may not be conscious but it goes on continually during the period of middle adolescence in a multitude of ways.

As might be expected, the problem of identity formation differs for boys and for girls. A major mechanism that boys use to establish their identity is to become increasingly independent of the family. A boy may take jobs away from home during the summer, spend weekends camping, and break away from routine family activities such as picnics and visits to friends. By establishing his independence, his right to make important decisions about his life, the boy gradually integrates the disparate facets of himself with the confidence that he is not only responsible for his fate but also has the strength and ability to direct it into productive channels and pathways.

Identity formation in girls, at least according to some researchers, comes about in a somewhat different fashion. For the girl, identity is not arrived at as much through establishing independence from the parents as it is by establishing intimacy with other people. The girl must learn social skills and must become aware of her feelings, learning how to control them and when to show them. Her sense of unique selfhood is thus likely to come from her sense of being a woman with a certain depth of understanding, sensitivity, and know-how in interpersonal relations. These social skills and the know-how not only help establish her identity as a woman, they also make her a formidable opponent when she is seeking a mate among the less socially sophisticated males.

The patterns of identity formation among young men and women will probably become more alike as adolescent girls begin to acquire the freedoms once accorded only to their brothers. Girls are likely to become more independent and self-sufficient than they have been in the past. This will inevitably bring about changes in the patterns of male-female interaction that, on balance, are likely to be to the good.

There are wide individual differences in the case with which adolescents attain a sense of personal identity. Some young people seem to establish a sense of personal identity smoothly and almost without effort. Other young people encounter much more difficulty. Some, for example, feel so overburdened and pressured by parents to adopt a ready-made identity that they adopt a "negative identity" by opposing everything the parents value. A white daughter of racist parents, to illustrate, will date only black young men. Or a boy from an orthodox Jewish family will date only Christian girls and attend church services. Such identities are in effect negatives of the positive identities held up by the parents as models to be followed.

Although most adolescents establish a sense of personal identity by the end of this transition period, it is never final or closed. One's sense of personal identity continues to change as one progresses through life and becomes a parent and a participant in community affairs. Certain aspects established in adolescence nevertheless remain relatively constant throughout life: the kind of person one believes oneself to be and the values and beliefs to which one is committed.

Social Development

Social relationships in adolescence show both continuity with childhood and manifestations that are unique to this period. In general, there are three major kinds of relationships in which young people are involved. Adolescents interact with their peers, with parents and other adults, and with groups of peers. While such relationships are already established in childhood, they take on a special coloration in adolescence, particularly because there is a divergence in the kinds of social relationships established by boys and girls. It makes sense, then, to consider the development of social relations in girls separately from the development of such relations in boys.

The friendship patterns of girls over the adolescent period follow a fairly regular course. Young adolescent girls tend to have one or more best friends from who they are inseparable and about whom they tend to be jealous. The loss of a friend of this sort is experienced as a very traumatic event. Towards middle adolescence the girl is likely to become part of a group of boys and girls who date, party, and "prom" together. The close ties with other girls is now lessened as attachments to boys become stronger. Towards the end of adolescence, although some girlhood friends are retained, the girl's prime commitment is usually to young men and the selection of a mate.

Girl-girl friendships in adolescence often have an exploitative quality. A pretty girl may have a plain girl as a friend who helps to set her off. The plain girl, in turn, gets vicarious satisfaction from living out in fantasy the exploits of her more fortunate friend. There is, moreover, always an underlying competitiveness among girls with respect to boys and always the suspicion that other girls will steal them away. Some girls engage in such "stealing" not because they are interested in the boys but in order to make the girls who were "stolen from" squirm. Although genuine friendships exist in adolescence (often these are based upon childhood acquaintance), many adolescent friendships do tend to be shallow and exploitative.

A somewhat similar developmental pattern appears among boys. They, too, develop close friendships with other boys and are jealous about them. At the same time, however, the young adolescent boy is likely to be a member of an informal group of boys who play ball, go bowling, or the like. In middle adolescence he also becomes a member of the heterosexual group and then later moves to almost exclusive pairing with a particular girl, although often in the company of friends who are dating other girls.

Like the friendships among girls, friendships among boys in adolescence can have an exploitative quality. The quiet boy befriends the boy with the bright personality, while the boy whose family has only one car befriends the boy who has his own car. However, boys do not appear to experience the same competitiveness that exists among girls. Acceptance and admiration by the opposite sex does not appear to be as crucial for the boy's self-concept and esteem as it is for the girl's because he has many other areas in which he can shine. There is no glitter among girls, however, that quite matches that of the girl whom young men find attractive.

According to psychoanalytic writers, adolescence is the period that sees the reawakening of the Oedipal conflict, wherein the young person loves the parent of the opposite sex and sees the same-sexed parent as a rival. This conflict is more powerful in adolescence because the young person is now sexually mature. Parents react in a similar fashion and have to work through their own problems in this area. Fathers who are unduly antagonistic towards their daughters' dates and mothers who react in a similar fashion to their sons' girl friends or who compete with their daughters reflect their involvement in the Oedipal-problem conflict.

In order to overcome this conflict, the adolescent has to find a new love object outside the family, and this results in new problems. As the adolescent begins to "fall in love" with members of the opposite sex, she feels that she must withdraw some of her love from her parents. This feeling derives from the mistaken notion that love is a fixed quantity, which must be withdrawn from one person in order to be given to another. (It takes more experience than the adolescent has had to discover that love defies the laws of conservation. The more love one gives, the more one has to give.) However, as a consequence of this feeling, the adolescent feels guilty towards her parents. To handle this guilt, she often seeks to find fault with the parents, since, if they are bad parents, they are not worthy of love, and hence she need not feel guilty about withdrawing love. Accordingly, many of the conflicts between parents and adolescents are "trumped up" in order to alleviate the adolescents' guilt.

The situation is, however, somewhat different for girls than it is for boys. Since very early childhood, the girl has always identified with her mother and shared her father as an object of love and admiration. Under these circumstances, it is more difficult for her to withdraw love from the mother and from the father. The girl, consequently, remains more closely tied to the family than does the boy. Frequently, for example, the girl does not move out of the family home until she is married, whereas this is less often true for the boy. The girl is, moreover, more likely to seek a mate similar to her father than the boy is to seek a mate similar to his mother.

On the boy's side, a different situation occurs. The boy's earliest identification, as for the girl, is with the mother, because the mother is usually the caretaking person. Towards the age of four or five, however, the boy must switch allegiance and begin to identify with the father as a role model. Accordingly, the boy has, early in his history, the experience of switching emotional attachments from one love object to another. Presumably this makes it easier for the adolescent boy, than for the adolescent girl, to break parental attachments and to seek independence. Society, of course, reinforces this pattern.

Sociocultural Change

The transition from childhood to adulthood always takes place in a particular sociocultural and historical context that to a large extent conditions the ease or difficulty with which the transition takes place. In certain primitive cultures, for example, where puberty is regarded as moving the young person into adult society, adolescence as we know it in Western culture does not exist. In such cultures childhood is preparation for adulthood, and puberty is the price of admission. Even a century ago in Western civilization, before the advent of child labor laws, the problem of adolescence did not exist for the children of working-class parents. Such children were treated as adults from the moment when they were strong enough to work.

Adolescence as we know it, the long transition between childhood and adult status, is largely a cultural invention. Modern society requires highly trained and technologically proficient persons to run a heavily automated way of life. The training of such people takes time. Moreover, in an industrialized society, where the routine jobs are taken over by machines, jobs are scarcer and the adolescents, were they not in school, would glut the labor market and, more likely than not, displace older workers. These are very real and significant reasons for the prolongation of adolescence in modern society. It is, in fact, an economic necessity.

While the prolongation of the adolescent period is essential from society's standpoint, it works hardships on young people. Physically able to work, procreate, and raise families, they must postpone these activities for at least several years. Furthermore, the education that they are offered during this period is not always appropriate to their interests or occupational needs. There are too few schools teaching trades and too many schools geared exclusively to the college-bound student. Many young people drop out of school for just that reason. They might have been willing to postpone going to work if school had offered them training in something they felt would further their vocational goals. But a girl going into auto mechanics is not likely to need French or foreign literature. While it would be nice if she wanted to learn these, in most cases she doesn't, and school might better teach her to be a skilled mechanic.

It is hard to predict how adolescence will be affected by today's rapid technological changes (including those in educational technology) or by its social changes, such as the increasing urbanization of America and the increasing segregation of American cities into black core and white suburban rings. If present trends continue, however, we are likely to see an accentuation of the tensions that already exist for young people.

These tensions exist, in part at least, because while the age of sexual maturity and sexual and social sophistication is going down, the age at which young people can enter the work force is going up. The demand is for more and more highly trained people, and such people command the highest salaries. But there is a need, too, for persons skilled in the trades, who also command high salaries. In today's job market, a college education is no longer a guarantee of a well-paying job.

It appears that the job situation will eventually level out as the number of persons entering the work force declines as a result of reduced family size. Couples are marrying later and having fewer children. The mean age of the population will grow older and, as a consequence, society as a whole will probably become less child centered.

General Characteristics of Adolescents

The interests of adolescents show both the continuity with the past and the preparation for the future that we have seen in other areas of adolescent behavior. Adolescent interests in activities, for example, tend to shift from solitary to group pursuits. The collections, model-building, sewing, and cooking activities so common during childhood are usually given up during adolescence. In their stead, young people participate in group sports or projects such as working on cars, building boats, or more group-oriented activities such as dancing and parties. The reading interests of adolescents exemplify this trend. Reading, which is a prime example of a solitary activity, tends to reach a peak at about the age of thirteen and to decline thereafter. Here again, however, it is well to remember that there are wide individual and social-class differences in this regard and that some young people continue to pursue their solitary activity interests far into adolescence.

One of the prime interests of adolescence is clothing. While girls are usually interested in clothing and in being neat and clean in childhood, this interest is relatively new for adolescent males, who were expected to be rather dirty and unkempt as boys. After about the age of thirteen or fourteen, however, boys become as clothes-conscious as girls and spend a lot of time before the mirror getting their clothing to fit just right. Having the right or "in" type of clothing is particularly important to adolescents, for whom such clothing is a badge of membership in the peer group. The girl who is not permitted to go braless today (it used to be tight sweaters) or the boy who is not permitted to wear skintight jeans (it used to be V-neck sweaters and loafer shoes) feels left out of things.

Vocational interests also become more prominent and realistic during the adolescent period. Whereas children think about future vocations in romantic terms—that is, of being like the policeman or fireman, whose uniform and car or truck is attractive and exciting—adolescents think about how they want to go about earning a living. Their vocational choices are, however, often temporary and may change as they meet new people, discover new vocations they had never known about (computer programming for example), and uncover hidden talents or abilities within themselves. While vocational interests tests are useful guides, they are far from infallible, and one of the best indices of what vocation is best suited to the young person is what he or she does in her or his spare time.

Closely related to interests are emotionally colored attitudes, or sets of ideas about the physical and social world.

Strong attitudes towards religious, ethnic, and racial groups frequently emerge in adolescence. Children, by and large, are free of prejudice and are likely to play with other children regardless of race, creed, or color. In adolescence, however, partly as a result of group pressure, there is distinct grouping along ethnic, racial, religious, and social-class lines. Young people tend to choose their closest friends from among those boys and girls who belong to the same church, ethnic group, and socioeconomic level. This group then becomes the "in group" and the others become the "out group." In general these groupings reflect parental prejudices that were acquired but remained latent during childhood. Such prejudices become manifest during adolescence, in part because the young person can now think in terms of general categories of people. In addition, when young people attain sexual maturity, and parental fears about marriage across racial, ethnic, religious, and social-class barriers are aroused, parents become more vocal and adamant about their prejudices.

In addition to these smaller, clique-type groups, the high school is likely to be divided into three larger groups, each of which has its own attitudes towards school and society and towards the other groups. Although these groups have different names in different geographic areas they are frequently termed the *socials* (those who dress well, date, have parties, and run school politics and organizations), the *grinds* (those concerned with getting good grades and with intellectual matters and pursuits, who tend to be solitary or to go with friends who have common interests), and the *baddies or hoods* (those who are uninterested in school, wear extreme forms of clothing, and tend to get into fights and into trouble with the law). The attitudes towards these various groups are so strong that it is often very difficult for a young person identified with one group to change and move into another group.

The difficulty young people encounter when they want to change their social group is evidenced by the case of one of my family court patients. This girl wanted to move from the "hood" group into the "social" group and began to change her style of dress, her speech, and her behavior. Although she met some initial resistance from the social group she began to be accepted. Then she got the flu and had to be out of school for several weeks. When she returned, the social group cut her cold. In the interim, her "friends" among the baddies had spread the rumor that she was pregnant and had gone away for an abortion. The girl then became truant and was removed to another school.

Despite their cliquish behavior and obvious prejudices, many adolescents become concerned about social issues such as racial discrimination, poverty, and political corruption. While they are highly critical of adult society in these regards and propose utopian solutions, their actions often belie their words. For, while they preach social action, they do not let these concerns interfere with their own pleasures, and their allowance continues to go for clothing, records, and dates rather than for social causes. Adolescents, no less than adults, spend a great deal of time talking about reform but devote little effort to doing anything about it. They behave as if to see a problem and to verbalize it, is tantamount to actually solving it. Theirs is an empty idealism bereft of the awareness of the practical actions needed to realize these ideals. It should be remembered, however, that this hypocrisy is only apparent and results from intellectual immaturity rather than from true moral blindness.

While adolescents profess liberal social ideals, their behavior is much more influenced by the peer group, particularly by the stars of the peer group (such as the rock-and-roll bands) who have been financially successful. It is not only the music that appeals to youth (and appeals, in part at least, because they consider it their own and because it drives adults into a frenzy) but also the fact that these young people have "made it" in adult society. The successful musical group epitomizes to adolescents that young people can sometimes beat adults at their own game.

In many respects the peer group is the single most important influence upon adolescents. It sets the style of clothing, the kinds of issues that are to be fought over with parents, and the kinds of social arrangements that are permissible. Going steady is sanctioned by some peer groups but not by others. In addition, the peer group sets the code for sexual behavior. Girls in the peer group quickly learn how far they are supposed to allow boys to go and how fast. Boys, in their turn, soon learn what and how much to expect from the girls. Young people who go too far or not far enough are either exiled from the groups or ridiculed. The use of alcohol and other drugs, so common today, is also peer-group initiated and perpetuated.

The prolongation of adolescence in our society has thus resulted in a youth culture with its own social hierarchy and prejudices, with its own music and language, and with its own codes of morals and ethics. The leaders of this culture are frequently those young people who have had artistic *and* financial success without being adults. While the culture of youth prides itself in being different from adult society in quality and in freedom, it is at least as conforming as adult society. Young people who do not go along with the language, clothes, and mores of the youth culture are simply ostracized. Youth culture, like adult culture, is fundamentally a mechanism for inducing and maintaining conformity.

The World of Self, Home, and Community

There is both continuity and change in the way in which the young person who has turned adolescent comes to view herself, her home, her school, and her community. She remains herself in temperament and in interpersonal style despite important changes in stature, voice, and appearance. Likewise, her parents are still her parents, and her siblings remain her siblings, and the affection she holds for them, although she shows it less, is not seriously altered by the fact of her becoming adolescent. The attitudes towards school that she developed in childhood are also carried over to junior high and high school. While there are sometimes dramatic changes in school performance during early adolescence, they are the exception rather than the rule. And while the adolescent begins to be more critical of her community, she still sees it as the backgound for many of her activities.

There are, however, significant changes as well. During adolescence the young person develops a true "sense of self." Although children are aware of themselves, they are not able to put themselves in other people's shoes and to look at themselves from that perspective. Adolescents can do this and engage in such self-watching to a considerable extent. Indeed, the characteristic "self-consciousness" of the adolescent period results from the very fact that the young person is now very much concerned with how others react to her. This is a concern that is largely absent in childhood. It helps to explain why some physically handicapped young people who were so surprisingly happy and well adjusted as children become depressed as adolescents.

Adolescent self-consciousness centers about appearance and, to a lesser extent, about personality, athletic prowess, and social skill. The concern of adolescents about acne, body odors, superfluous hair, and body proportions is hard to exaggerate. Although it may seem silly to adults, it is very important to young people. The hours spent before the mirror, the money spent on salves and creams to hide acne and to deodorize, and the excruciating diets and bodybuilding exercises engaged in by adolescents all attest to this tremendous preoccupation with the body and to a heightened self-consciousness. They also explain the young person's hypersensitivity to any even slightly derogatory or teasing remark about her face or figure. In general, this hyper-self-consciousness diminishes as the adolescent grows older and becomes better adapted to her changed appearance.

Although the adolescent continues to view her parents and siblings with affection, she now begins to look at them with a more critical eye. Just as she is now able to see herself from the perspective of other people, she can now look at her home as others view it and frequently she finds it wanting. If her parents speak with an accent, belong to a far-out religious sect, or don't behave in a way that adolescents believe they should, the family comes in for strong criticism. Even when the family conforms reasonably well to the community stereotype, the adolescent may feel that her father's occupation does not have the status of her friends' and feel embarrassed if her father is a plumber rather than an accountant. On the other hand, some adolescents may be critical of their parents for being too successful and for being too materialistic. During this critical phase in early adolescence, it is hard for the parents to be entirely acceptable no matter who or what they are.

Younger, as well as older, brothers and sisters also come under new scrutiny at this time. The young adolescent feels closer to her older siblings than to the younger ones with whom she was formerly grouped. The younger members of the family are now viewed as a nuisance and a bother, whereas older siblings are now emulated. Whereas during childhood sibling fights were usually over toys and prerogatives, in adolescence they often center around clothing and activities (such as the younger sibling's wish to "tag along" with the older sibling). As the young person becomes adolescent, her younger sisters and brothers become "kids," and she looks at them with a critical eye and doesn't hesitate to comment on their cleanliness, eating habits, and manners. Here again, the adolescent is thinking about the impression her younger siblings are going to make upon her friends.

During adolescence, then, the young person begins to look at her home and family from the outside in. Because she is so very concerned with making an impression and with how other people will react to her home and family, she becomes hypercritical. Features of family life that the child accepted without question now become points of contention. Father should not wear those old, paint-stained trousers and mother ought not to wear shorts, and so on. Here, again, as the adolescent matures and becomes less concerned with impressions and more concerned with people as people, her criticism of her parents diminishes, and in young adulthood she begins to appreciate her parents as individuals rather than as "appearances."

Adolescence brings with it new freedoms and opportunities to explore the community and its resources for young people. Whereas the center for the activities of childhood is in the home, during adolescence it often switches to a candy store, drugstore, pizza kitchen, ice-cream parlor, or shopping mall, where young people can congregate after school. In addition, now that the adolescent can go to places like movies and swimming pools on her own, she begins to come into direct contact with the community. Certain areas of the community in particular tend to become associated with adolescent groups and activities.

This new interaction between young people and the community is not always harmonious. Young people feel the community ought to provide places for them to congregate, and if it does not, they make their own place. If the community and business people are cooperative, this can work well, but the noisy rowdiness so typical of young adolescents makes many businessmen dread the adolescent trade. In addition, a good many young people steal from local stores for the excitement and as a way of showing their disdain of adult authority and rules. There have been cases in which stores have closed because the amount of theft made commerce an unprofitable venture. Interestingly, when the community has provided facilities for youth, such facilities have often been used for only a short time. Apparently, adolescents want to choose their own places to congregate.

Her perspective of the school also changes when the young person reaches adolescence. During childhood, school is seen as primarily a place for academic activities, and the organization of the elementary school, a single group in a single classroom for an entire day, adds to this orientation. In adolescence, however, the school takes on a new dimension. It now becomes a place for socialization, for watching, and for being seen. It becomes the place for violent crushes and bitter feuds and not a few out-and-out fights. The mobility of the junior high and high school students who move from class to class heightens these social aspects of the school. In the school, cliques and groups form and the patterns of social ostracism and acceptance begin that find full fruition in young adulthood. During adolescence, then, the school becomes much more than a place of learning; rather, it becomes a stage on which much of the drama of adolescent friendships, rivalries, and hostilities take place and find their fullest expression.

Just as adolescents acquire a changed perspective of themselves, their homes, communities, and schools, so these various institutions look on adolescents differently than they do on children. Most often the attitudes these institutions take toward youth are reactions to adolescent behavior rather than reflections of deep-seated prejudices. Therefore, the perspective of parents, school, and community to adolescent youth tends to be defensive and retaliatory rather than malicious.

Parents who suffer the verbal attacks of their offspring are likely to become defensive and to feel that their children are ungrateful. They may complain that their children are getting too "picky" and critical, and say if the young people don't like it they can move out and find better parents. Siblings who suddenly come within range of adolescent guns find that their former cohorts against the parents are now more critical and demanding than the parents themselves. Younger siblings are less vulnerable, however, and more able to sense the insecurity upon which the adolescents' criticism is based. Accordingly, they are likely to shrug off the criticism and even to make fun of and tease the exaggerations of their older brothers and sisters.

As suggested earlier, the community's attitude towards young people changes as they begin to congregate in particular areas. In general, the community tends to view young people as an unstable group in their midst that they must tolerate, although not without raised eyebrows and grimaces about adolescent clothing, music, and uninhibited behavior. Of course, not all adolescents behave in this way, but the visible (and audible) minority rather than the quiet majority tends to attract community attention. Unfortunately, the community is all too ready to generalize from the few loud youngsters to all young people. Perhaps adults overreact to adolescents because they are themselves feeling the pressures of age. Consequently, they resent the way some adolescents publicly flaunt their youth, strength, and sexual attractiveness.

The school, too, looks differently upon the adolescent than it does upon the child. More rules about dress and behavior are laid down, and more restrictions are placed upon behavior. At the same time, the school recognizes the social needs of young people and tries to provide for dances and intramural sports that help to channel and fill the social needs of its students. The provision of a more flexible curriculum and the opportunity to select courses and areas of study reflect the school's awareness that the adolescent is now capable of making decisions about her future and of taking some responsibility for it.

The adolescent, then, comes to view herself, her home, her school, and her community differently as she becomes self-conscious and socially oriented. Home, school, and community, in turn, look at adolescents differently than they do at children. Often this change is in response to the youth offensive and is consequently defensive in character. Probably the least disturbed by the adolescent onslaught are younger siblings, who are not only less vulnerable than parents but who are also better able to see through the adolescent criticism and to discern the underlying insecurity about self that dictates so much of adolescent criticism of home, school, and community.

Adolescents in Relation to Adults

In talking about the relationship between adolescents and adults we have to distinguish between the individual relationship between particular adolescents and their parents on the one hand and between adolescents as a group and adults as a society on the other. While the problems on the individual and group levels are sometimes parallel, there are also problems that are unique to one or the other. Therefore, these two types of relationship need to be dealt with separately.

On an individual basis, the way in which an adolescent relates to an adult will depend upon a host of factors, including the kinship relationship between the two, their sex, the age of the adolescent, and the maturity of the adult. The relationship will also vary with the social class and with the culture of the young person involved. In discussing the adolescent's approach to the adult, we will be talking primarily about the middle-class adolescent in American society.

Adolescents in Relation to Their Parents

The relationship between adolescents and their parents is best characterized by the term *ambivalence*. The ambivalence of the adolescent vis-à-vis her parents extends into many different areas and goes in many different directions. It is this ambivalence that is, for example, often at the heart of many parent-child conflicts. Some of the adolescent areas of ambivalence are described below.

Adolescents are, first of all, ambivalent about growing up. While growing up holds many attractions in terms of freedom, it also holds many negative consequences. It means taking on responsibility and earning a living. In addition, it means growing older and perhaps getting fat and bald or losing shapely curves. Likewise, growing up means giving up many of the special prerogatives of childhood, such as being special and being entirely involved in the present rather than in the future. There is a little of the child in every adolescent, and this contributes to her ambivalence about growing up. With respect to parents this means that the adolescent expects to be treated as an adult or as a child at her discretion. This leaves most parents wobbling, since they are not always sure how to treat their offspring.

Closely related to this adult-child ambivalence is another that has to do with independence and dependence. While the adolescent very much wants to be independent she at the same time doesn't want to give up her dependence. She wants to be independent when it comes to deciding how late she will stay out at night, what clothes she will wear, and what friends she will travel with. At the same time she wants parents to provide the money and car for her dates, take care of her clothing and sport equipment needs, and clean up her room and wash her clothing. The adolescent can be, moreover, quite erratic in her demands for independence. One moment she will ask parents to make a decision and the next moment she will tell the parent not to interfere.

Still another area of ambivalence is that of sexuality. While the boy wants to date girls and "make out," she is often still ambivalent about this sort of activity. Many boys have a sort of "sacred-profane" attitude towards girls. Some girls are for sexual exploitation whereas others, modeled after mother and sister, are to be revered and respected. The adolescent boy's ambivalence about sexual activity, then, derives in part from his tendency to regard some girls as similar to the women in his family and to regard sexual activity as a violation of a taboo.

A young woman's ambivalence about sexuality has a somewhat different basis. She is under tremendous pressure from parents to refrain from sexual activity, and she may suffer fears and anxieties derived from peculiar ideas about insemination. A not infrequent fantasy, for example, is that kissing can cause pregnancy. Even though a girl may be interested in sexual activity, she may inhibit her response because of her parents, fear for her reputation, and fear of what the boy might think of her if she shows her affection or goes too far in the petting-kissing sequence. The girl's ambivalence about sexual activity centers, then, not about the object of her affections, as in the case of the boy, but rather about the consequences of her behavior in relation to her parents and her reputation. Even in today's relatively enlightened age, these patterns tend to persist.

Adolescents in Relation to Nonparental Adults

When adolescents deal with adults outside the family they are likely to react in several characteristic ways. One way is to treat all adults as if they were merely extensions of the parents. The browbeaten girl who obeys parents without question may respond in the same manner to all adult authority. Contrariwise, the girl who rebels against a father who is too authoritarian may assume that all men are this way and respond accordingly. Boys, too, may recapitulate the conflicts they have with their mothers with every adult woman they encounter.

A somewhat different reaction is to treat adults as the opposites of parents: that is, to idealize them. The crushes that an adolescent sometimes get on a teacher or other adult is often based on the adolescent's belief that the adult epitomizes all that the parents lack in the way of understanding, kindness, and sensitivity. Many adolescents, to illustrate, are closer to their friends' parents or to uncles or aunts than they are to their own parents. These nonparental adults can often be of considerable value to the adolescent provided they do not further undermine the parents and do not accept all the negatives about parents that adolescents are willing to expound. In my work with adolescents I have found that it is sometimes useful to agree with a young person's negative evaluation of his or her parents. "Yes" I sometimes say, "It sounds like you really got stuck with a couple of bummers, better luck next time." When responded to in this way, many adolescents come to the defense of their parents. Clearly this approach has to be used with caution but it can help the adolescent discover some of the positive attributes of parents.

Still another approach of adolescents to adults is to assume that adults are so different and far out that it is impossible to communicate with them. It is the "you can't trust anyone over thirty" attitude. Adults are simply "square." Adolescents frequently see adults as people to be "bugged" and take a certain pleasure in alarming adults by their speech, clothing, and potentially destructive behavior. In such situations there is a great deal of mutual hostility and fear. The adolescent sees the adult as the enemy who has a powerful army that he can combat only with guerrilla tactics. Adults, on their side, are angry and frightened by the attacks of youth but are not prepared to fight the kind of war that adolescents are waging.

Adolescents and Adult Society

The relation of adolescents to the larger society is again marked by ambivalence. Adolescents want to be treated as a group in their own right and do not like being grouped with children, as they often are. While young people feel loyalty to their country and community, they also feel that the country and community have not taken sufficient account of their talents and abilities. Young people today want more of a say in how things should be run; they want to help make the decisions that will affect their future. Increasingly they are coming to the conclusion that they can no longer trust adults to manage the future because adults are no longer committed to youth.

Adults in Relation to Adolescents

As was true for the relation of adolescents to adults, the relation of adults to adolescents must be considered separately for individual parents and their offspring and for adult society and the youth culture. For, while there are many similarities, there are also many differences.

Parents and Their Adolescents

When we look at the relation between parents and their adolescents we observe that adults, too, are ridden by ambivalences. For one thing, parents are ambivalent about their children's growing up. While they take pride and pleasure in seeing them grow and in seeing their accomplishments, this growth also makes the parents not a little sad. The cuddly child is no more, and it is hard to fondle a hefty six-footer. Moreover, the growing up of children is clear evidence that the parents themselves are getting older and may soon be grandparents. Finally, children's growth means that they will probably soon leave the home. To many parents, the coming of age of their offspring signals a new downswing in their own lives.

Parents are equally ambivalent about granting their adolescents independence. Although they are happy to see their children take responsibiltiy, they have new anxieties when adolescents are driving the car or going off for weekend outings. There is, moreover, a certain sadness about having to give up control and power over children. As parents lose this power, they may be bereft of a sense of importance and relevance in their children's lives.

In the areas of sexuality, ambivalence on the part of parents is equally prominent. Parents want their children to be popular socially and to be involved in dating and party behavior. But there is a little resentment as well. Fathers don't like to think of boys fondling their daughters and mothers don't like to think of their sons in the hands of scheming females. Parents of girls fear that the girls might get into trouble, and such fear makes parents much stricter about girls' behavior than about the behavior of boys.

Parents, then, are ambivalent about their offspring's growing up, becoming independent, and engaging in sexual activities. The ambivalence is often expressed in inconsistent and seemingly illogical behavior on the part of parents. A sudden wave of self-pity may lie behind a mother's refusal to let her son go on an outing against which she would, at other times, have no objections. Likewise, a father might decide not to let his son use the car in order to exercise a power he suddenly feels is slipping away from him. Parents can be as erratic and arbitrary in their behavior as their adolescent offspring.

In dealing with adolescents the cardinal rule is *not to make rules that one cannot enforce.* It is really impossible to prohibit a young person from smoking marijuana or drinking beer. All that one can reasonably do is express one's feelings and explain why one believes the behavior is not a good idea. It is, for example, against the law. But it is senseless to prohibit such behavior because it is really impossible for the parent to enforce this prohibition.

Nonparental Adults and Adolescents

When we look at the relation of nonparental adults to adolescents, there is tremendous variation. Some adults feel threatened and terrorized by young people, and their very fear tends to evoke new threatening behaviors on the part of youth. Other adults are genuinely interested in young people and make it their business to befriend and help them. By and large, however, the majority of adults who have no direct contact with adolescents tend to look on them as something of a curiosity and as fair game for criticism and derision.

As we turn now to adult society's relations to adolescents we observe some unhappy circumstances. On the whole, society tends to treat adolescents pretty much as if they were children. The laws for drinking, purchase of cigarettes, and attendance at adult movies all specify an age towards the end of adolescence. The only concession in this regard is the age for attaining a driving license, which is sixteen in many states. From the strictly legal point of view, therefore, adult society often lumps adolescents and children together without paying due regard to the differences between these two age periods.

However, adult society does not always treat adolescents like children. When it comes to marketing new products, business becomes acutely aware of differences between children and adolescents with respect to taste in clothes, foods, and so on. The sales pitch to adolescents also takes account of the differences between adolescent and child interests and modes of thought. Accordingly, adult society can take account of the distinction between adolescents and children but does this usually only when it is economically expedient and not necessarily when it is socially relevant.

The picture of adult society vis-à-vis adolescent youth is, therefore, not a very pretty picture. Society has placed adolescents in the fix they are in and does not really know what to do about the situation. To be sure, most young people muddle through adolescence without lasting scars. They find a cause, a hobby, a profession that gives their lives meaning and direction. They find some continuity between past and future by engaging in some form of productive work. Other young people, however, begin drinking and taking drugs at a relatively early age because, in part at least, society has not helped them to make the painful transition from childhood to adulthood. The alarming increase in delinquent behavior in our cities is but one sign of the necessity for communities to recognize that adolescents are not children and that many need help in finding meaningful work that will prepare them to become productive members of adult society.

10 Mental Development

In general, intelligence has to do with knowing and with the processes by which knowledge is acquired, retained, and put to use. As the child grows older and moves into adolescence her intellectual abilities grow too. Indeed, the growth in mental ability that occurs in adolescence equals, in extent, the changes that occur in the adolescent's body, appearance, and personality. Just as there is a physical growth spurt in adolescence, so does there appear to be a corresponding spurt in mental ability.

The changes that take place in adolescents' mental prowess are quantitative and qualitative and have to do with both the amount and the kinds of knowledge and mental abilities that adolescents have at their disposal. As measured by intelligence tests, many mental abilities reach their quantitative peak of proficiency during adolescence. It is not necessarily true, however, that intelligence begins a progressive decline after the adolescent years. Whether particular mental powers are maintained at a high level in adulthood very much depends upon the kind of mental ability in question, the occupation of the person, her overall level of intelligence, and many other factors.

Another quantitative aspect of mental growth during adolescence has to do with the differentiation of mental abilities and knowledge acquisition. Whereas mental growth during childhood is relatively even, during adolescence some mental abilities are more developed than others, depending upon the individual. Recent data, for example, suggest a relationship between the rate of maturation and mental ability. Early-maturing boys and girls are better at verbal skills than are late-maturing boys and girls. But late-maturing boys and girls are better at spatial abilities than are early-maturing boys and girls. If girls tend, on the average, to be better in verbal abilities but worse in spatial skills, it may be because they usually mature earlier than boys do.

The differentiation and specialization of knowledge (as opposed to ability), however, is probably not due to any innate differences between boys and girls with respect to rate of maturation or aptitude. The truth is much more likely that in our culture boys are expected to do well in science and mathematics and girls are supposed to be good in verbal skills. It is probably the social pressures to conform to sexual stereotypes that cause many girls to fail in math when they could easily have mastered the subject. In addition, girls discover that intellectual competition with boys is not the road to dates and popularity. The poor marks attained by boys in English probably derive in part from the notion that there is something of the "sissy" in a boy who studies language arts.

Still another quantitative aspect of intellectual growth has to do with the continuity of a young person's intellectual standing across time. Does the boy who is the brightest youngster in his second-grade class remain in that position during tenth grade? Likewise, does the girl who is in the middle of the group have any chance of shooting to the top later? The answer is a complex one. By and large the intellectual standing of a child relative to her classmates tends to remain about the same from childhood to adolescence. This is not always true, however, since children as a result of changed life circumstances can suddenly blossom intellectually. It is also true that some young people who have done very well in grade school begin to do very poorly in high school, either because of personal problems, running around with adolescents uninterested in school, or other reasons. So, while a child's intellectual standing relative to her classmates does tend to remain the same, remarkable changes in both directions can and do occur.

When we turn to the qualitative aspects of mental growth we see both continuity with the past and new changes that herald the future. Although the child is able to reason and solve problems, her reasoning and problem-solving abilities are limited in a very important respect. While she can reason about things, she cannot reason about verbal propositions. To illustrate, if a child is shown three blocks that vary in size, she can, without comparing them directly, deduce that if A is bigger than B and B is bigger than C, then A is bigger than C. At the same time, however, if she is asked, "If Helen is taller than Doris, and Doris is taller than Elaine, who is the tallest of the three?" she cannot answer, although it merely puts into words the problem with the blocks. The adolescent can answer this question.

In addition to being able to reason about verbal propositions, the adolescent is able to introspect and to examine her own thinking. During adolescence young people talk for the first time about their minds, beliefs, ideas, and hunches. At the same time, however, they realize that their thoughts are private and that they can say one thing while they are thinking another. The adolescent is thus more tactful than the child, who says whatever pops into her mind, but is also more given to dissimulation and to intentional manipulations of the truth.

Another feature of adolescent reasoning is the ability to understand metaphor. Children do not understand metaphor because they are very literal in their interpretation of language. A child has difficulty, for example, in grasping that the term *rat* or *dog* can be applied to people because she can't grasp that a person can be like a rat or dog in some respects and not in others. That is why children do not get the point of political or other types of satirical cartoons. It is also why they do not grasp the metaphorical social significance of stories like *Gulliver's Travels* and *Alice in Wonderland*. Adolescents, however, are able to grasp the deeper meanings imbedded in these metaphorical tales.

The adolescent's grasp of metaphor considerably expands her range of understanding. She no longer takes everything literally and begins to sense the multiple meanings inherent in a given word, picture, or gesture. Her new awareness of multiple meanings and possibilities, however, may lead to a certain intellectual indecisiveness and hesitancy. Once she can appreciate the possibility of a multiplicity of meanings and interpretations she has difficulty in deciding what meaning was actually intended. Questions posed by adolescents sometimes appear bullheaded because young people may have difficulty in understanding just what was meant by a particular remark or statement.

In addition to being able to grasp metaphor, the adolescent can, for the first time, think in terms of ideals and of contrary-to-fact conditions. She can begin to think of all possible situations and events and, hence, of those that have never existed. This is in contrast to the child, who lives in the present and who is concerned with what is, rather than with what might be.

If a child is told, "Let's suppose today is Monday," she is likely to reply, "But today is Saturday," whereas the adolescent can accept the contrary-to-fact proposition and reason from it.

The adolescent's ability to think in terms of ideals and contrary-to-fact conditions has very important consequences. Not only does it permit her to begin planning realistically for the future but it also is the basis for the new perspective on her home, family, school, and community. Now, for example, she can compare her parents with ideal mothers and fathers. When the adolescent does that, she often finds her parents sadly wanting in comparison with the ideal parents, and this dissatisfaction often becomes an issue in the conflict between herself and her own mother and father.

It also becomes an issue within herself, because she can now distinguish between her real self and her ideal self — the person she would like to be. The ideal self plays a role in the dieting, weight-lifting, and exercising that so many adolescents engage in. Many young people try to change not only their faces and figures but also their personalities in order to come into greater conformity with what they consider ideal. Even attractive young people who serve as ideals for other adolescents may have reservations about their appearances or personalities.

Adolescents exhibit equally remarkable changes in their problem-solving skills. This is best illustrated in comparison with the problem-solving of children. In one study, for example, both children and adolescents read a paragraph about Stonehenge, in England, where certain arrangements of boulders are believed to be the work of primitive man. Both children and adolescents were asked to judge, on the basis of the information given, whether the formations were created as a fort or as a religious shrine.

The answers given by children revealed that they based their decision upon a single bit of evidence. When this interpretation was challenged, however, they did not change the interpretation but instead tried to reevaluate the facts. Put differently, they tried to alter the facts to fit the interpretation, rather than the reverse. Adolescents, on the contrary, immediately gave up an interpretation that seemed counter to the evidence and devised a new interpretation. In short, children do not appear to distinguish clearly between their hypotheses and the facts and assume that both have the same priority; adolescents give priority to facts over hypotheses because they are aware of the difference between their own guesses and the facts of the case.

Accordingly, in problem-solving situations adolescents can raise and test hypotheses in a systematic way. This skill is basic to all scientific thinking. However, while the adolescent can use her problem-solving skills in the physical world, she does not automatically carry them over to the social world. Long after she is testing hypotheses in physics and chemistry, the adolescent is still responding to first impressions in social situations and altering facts to fit these impressions. The expression "love is blind" is another way of describing the fact that even adolescents and adults can occasionally revert to making the facts fit the hypotheses rather than the reverse.

Not only is the adolescent able to distinguish between facts and hypotheses, she is also able to deal with complex problems involving many factors simultaneously. Such thinking is required in science, where, for example, the impact of a moving object will depend upon its mass, its rate of speed, and the object that it hits. In order for any one of these variables to be studied, the others have to be held constant, but the young person must be aware that the impact is a result of all the factors involved. Children can deal with situations in which two factors play a part, but it is only in adolescence that the young person can deal with causal situations in which there are multiple determinants.

So far we have spoken about adolescence in general without attempting to distinguish ages within that period. Young adolescents (ages twelve to thirteen) do differ from middle adolescents (ages fourteen to fifteen) in significant respects in both the cognitive and the social spheres. By and large the young adolescent tends to be rather flighty as a consequence of the rapid changes that have been occurring in her. Because the changes are new she is more preoccupied with them than she will be later when she is more accustomed to her adult body and awakened sexual interest and curiosity.

The young person has to adjust not only to the new changes in her body, but also to new changes in her thinking abilities. Certain phenomena of early adolescence reflect this adjustment period. As we have noted, the twelve- and thirteen-year-old can now deal with possibilities and consider many new alternatives in any given problem-solving situation. Initially this is a somewhat terrifying experience because while the young person can see the many possible alternatives, she does not have the background or experience upon which to base a choice. It often appears, as a consequence, that young adolescents are hopelessly dependent and indecisive.

The situation is not really that different from the young child in the candy store who, confronted with all the varieties of candy, cannot quite make up her mind about what she wants to purchase. The child, however, has all the alternatives presented for her; she has only to choose, not to construct the alternatives. The adolescent must, however, not only choose but also construct the alternatives. For example, the young adolescent may search for ways to spend the summer, but then have to debate whether to get a job, go to summer school, go to camp, or just stay around the house. Often the solution is reached by default and the young person stays around the house, not particularly because she wanted to, but because she couldn't decide among the alternatives. By the age of fifteen and sixteen, however, young people have had more experience in decision-making and have a better idea of the relative importance of things. Accordingly, older adolescents are more independent and less indecisive than they were a few years before.

Just as the young adolescent has trouble adjusting to her new ability to consider multiple alternatives, so does she have trouble in dealing with her new ability to construct ideals and to think of contrary fact conditions. The young adolescent first senses this power of idealization in the area of home and family. Her parents are the first to be compared with "other" more ideal parents and to be found wanting. Her house, neighborhood, and siblings are also compared with others, and the young person feels critical and, not uncommonly, envious of friends who have more "ideal" parents and homes. In early adolescence not only is the grass greener in the other person's yard, but the house is bigger and more comfortable and the parents are nicer.

The young adolescent's critical eye is also turned towards the school and the teacher. Whereas children may not like a teacher, they are seldom critical of him or her as a teacher. They assume that he or she knows the material to be taught. Very quickly, however, the young adolescent becomes critical of the teacher's knowledge and ability as well as of his or her personality. She is less concerned with how nice the teacher is than with whether or not he or she knows the subject. This focus upon the teacher's knowledge puts a new strain on teacher-student relations, because young adolescents touch on a very sensitive area, the teacher's professional competence.

Towards middle adolescence, young people begin to be more concerned with general social issues and a little less concerned with the family and school as subjects of criticism. Now society, the church, and many social institutions begin to be looked at more critically, as are other countries and other peoples. This does not mean necessarily that the tension between parents and adolescents and teachers and adolescents diminishes, but the criticism becomes more widespread and is, therefore, a little more diluted than it was earlier.

This change of focus of interest from home and school to the larger society and to other countries is a general trend in the development from young to middle adolescence. As the young adolescent gradually overcomes the self-centeredness occasioned by the new bodily changes of puberty, she increasingly turns her attention outward to new people and to other issues and begins to seek new models after which to pattern her style of personal identity. She becomes, at the same time, both more objective and more subjective—more objective in the sense that she can turn her new mental abilities to topics and issues (such as foreign affairs) unrelated to herself, and more subjective in the sense that she is aware of her own limitations in learning about and understanding these new topics and issues.

11 Age Profiles

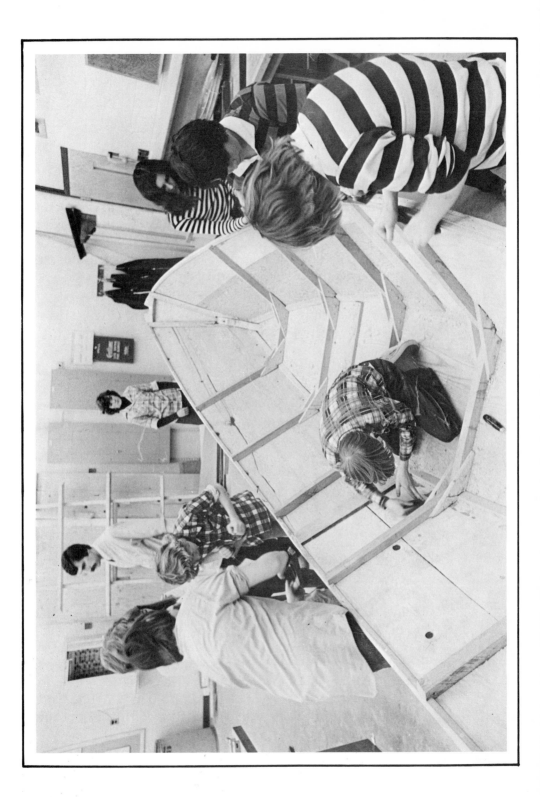

All of the comments made in the preface to the age profiles of infants and children pertain equally well to the age-wise descriptions of adolescents. The age profiles below are to be taken as averages and not as standards against which to assess the goodness or badness of a child's development. Such a use of these age norms would be opposed to their central aim, which is to provide a sympathetic understanding of young people.

The Twelve-Year-Old

The usual twelve-year-old tends to be outgoing, enthusiastic, and generous. His emotions tend to go to extremes; when he likes something he likes it very much indeed and when he dislikes something he really hates it. The twelve-year-old is still relatively uncomplicated emotionally, and parents and other adults tend to find him open, friendly, and endowed with a sense of humor that allows him to laugh at himself and to give and take in humorous insult and practical jokes.

Looking at the twelve-year-old's self-concept, we find that he is beginning to assert that he is no longer a child. At this age he often tries to find and define himself by forming friendships and in this way establishes the fact that he is capable of being liked by people other than his family. He is just beginning to be able to get outside himself and to look at himself and his family more objectively, but he has not yet reached the stage of social criticism. He is less self-centered, but his behavior may be erratic and he may show rapid shifts from relatively mature to relatively childish modes of behavior. He is rather critical of his appearance at this stage and may have difficulty accepting praise, under which he squirms or clowns.

Most twelve-year-olds relate successfully to peers and adults. Children of this age get along reasonably well with fathers, although the relationship may be less close than it was during childhood proper. Daughters often develop a flirtatious new worshipping attitude toward father and feel closer to him than ever before. Nonetheless, twelve-year-olds participate less in family activities than they did as children, a trend that becomes increasingly evident at later age levels. At this age, too, young people are aware of the criticism of their parents towards them and they in turn begin to make joking criticisms of their parents. They may, for example, tease father about his bald spot or paunch. There is also likely to be a new competitiveness with parents, both in sports and in intellectual games.

By the age of twelve many girls are romantically interested in boys, but this interest is usually expressed in a tremendous amount of talk. A girl frequently expresses a liking for a boy whom she feels is her "boy friend" even when the boy may be quite unaware of the girl's interest in him. There is still little dating at this age, and some twelve-year-old girls still think of boys as frightful creatures. Interest in making friends with girls is very great at this stage, and friendships are more or less indiscriminate with girls being able to get along with almost any other girl. There is a great emphasis upon best friends and also considerable complaining about friends. But the twelve-year-old girl is an eager friend-maker.

Boys at twelve are beginning to be interested in girls and many claim to have a "girl friend." As was true for the girls, however, the "girl friend" in question is often unaware of her status. At this age the dominant mode of direct interaction between boys and girls is still "play." Twelve-year-old boys have many boy friends and take pride in the number of their best friends. There are fights and arguments and considerable shifting about of friendships, but the twelve-year-old is usually friends with somebody most of the time.

The reading preferences of the twelve-year-olds tend towards sports, adventures, and classics. They don't like love stories, and think animal stories childish. Television-watching is less extensive than it was even a year ago. Some twelve-year-olds are already tired of westerns and prefer mysteries and comedy programs. Similar preferences hold for movie-going, which is relatively infrequent. Children at this age may, however, see the same picture over and over again if they really like it. Twelve-year-old boys are very sports-minded and may follow professional sports avidly. Girls, on the other hand, often begin to lose interest in sports at about this age, although this is far less true today than it was when female participation in team sports was much more limited because of sex-role stereotyping.

With respect to schooling, twelve-year-olds are likely to take strong stands and claim either to hate school or to love it. There is frequently a lot of restlessness, daydreaming, and general fooling around. Although children at this age will respond to a strong teacher, a teacher who lacks skill can easily lose control of the class, which quickly becomes chaos. It is generally difficult to get twelve-year-old children to work together as a group because each one is so interested in expressing himself or herself that true classroom coordination is precluded. This disruptive classroom behavior, it should be emphasized, expresses the attributes of twelve-year-olds and does not necessarily express a dislike for school or for the teacher.

The Thirteen-Year-Old

In many thirteen-year-olds there appears to be a gradual turning inward and preoccupation with self and self-evaluation. The thirteen-year-old is frequently "touchy." At this age the young person is likely to sulk and go to her room when angry or upset or, less frequently, to respond with sarcastic remarks. The thirteen-year-old often enjoys the errors and mistakes of others. Boys and girls at this age often seem to have more "worries" than fears, which was not true at younger age levels. In general, thirteen seems to be a period of introspection and appears to be the least happy of the adolescent years, perhaps because at this age young people are more sensitive to real or imagined slights.

Thirteen's introspectiveness also appears in her search for a personal self and self-understanding. At this age the adolescent agonizes over being too fat, or too short, too tall, or too weak. Young people during this period are very concerned about being like other members of their group in dress and behavior. There is also emphasis on inner qualities such as "brains" and "personality." At thirteen boys and girls like to keep to themselves as they discover the privacy of their own thoughts. Attempts of adults and siblings to talk to them are often regarded as prying. It is important to realize that thirteen's reclusiveness is a constructive and necessary period of inner consolidation that requires a certain freedom from external intrusions.

The seclusiveness of the average thirteen-year-old is frequently associated with a diminution of friendships, which are less close than they were before. Girls tend to form threesomes, and frequently two of the girls will gossip about the third in her absence. Interest in friends may vary from day to day, and friends are seen mostly as those to whom secrets can be confided. Boys, too, seem to have fewer friends at thirteen and are more easily angered and upset by other boys. Although some group activities persist, even fairly close groups may split up, with each boy going his own way.

Some girls may begin dating at thirteen, but this is more the exception than the rule. Again, there are still some girls at thirteen to whom boys are poison. However, most girls at this age are romantically interested in boys and talk a lot about them but without being "boy-crazy." The fact that many girls are larger than boys at this age creates a problem in boy-girl relations. Thirteen-year-old girls may be more critical of boys than they were at twelve but some still act silly and giggle when boys are around.

Boys show less interest in girls when they are thirteen than when they were twelve. Although they continue to be interested in girls, they are not so concerned about acknowledging a particular girl as a "girl friend." Few thirteen-year-old boys date girls and some are confirmed woman-haters. The forms of boy-girl interaction are still childish, and boys at this age may still grab a girl's hat or wrest away her books, or tease and plague her in other ways.

Perhaps as a consequence of the inner directiveness of the thirteen-year-old, reading tends to increase, and favorite books are read and reread. Favorite books are those that involve a lot of action, such as detective, adventure, and mystery stories. Many young people at this age still read comic books. At the same time that reading increases, television-watching decreases and there is less devotion to particular programs. Television is now looked on as a distraction, and there is less concern about what is being watched. Movie-going and telephoning are more frequent at thirteen than they were at age twelve. Interest in outdoor activities is greater among boys, who tend to enjoy sports more than girls do. Although more and more girls are getting involved in team sports, for many girls riding bikes and walking are still their major outdoor activities.

Within the school setting, boys and girls are more settled than they were at twelve, perhaps because they are getting used to the freedom of moving from class to class and can make the transitions with less disruption. In general, youngsters at this age are better organized and use their time more efficiently than they did before. Because of their concern with their individuality, many thirteen-year-olds appreciate special projects and activities that reflect their unique personalities. At the same time, the thirteen-year-old may be shy and unwilling to read or perform in front of her classmates. Although adolescents can be critical of their teachers at this age level, they still want and need direction. At this age, too, they are beginning to distinguish between a teacher's ability to teach and their own personal like or dislike of the teacher as a person.

The Fourteen-Year-Old

By the age of fourteen many young people have moved out of the introspective reclusive stage characteristic of age thirteen. At this age young people become more outgoing and happy and are less sensitive and "touchy" than they were a year earlier. At fourteen the young person gets along better with parents, siblings, and other adults and seems more mature and self-confident. It is likely that the inwardness of the thirteen-year-old was a necessary phase in the preparation for the new maturity of age fourteen.

In a sense, the fourteen-year-old has largely worked through many of his anxieties about growing up and rushes to meet life with enthusiasm. He is happy much more often than he is sad. Occasionally, to be sure, there are intense emotional flare-ups, but young people at this age get over these upsets fairly easily. At fourteen, too, adolescents are much more open about expressing their feelings and are not afraid to show anger or affection. Fears and worries are fewer and more specific than at age thirteen, and most young people at this age have "pet" fears and "pet" worries. Perhaps most characteristic of this is the light humorous touch shown in gifts and remarks that reveal that fourteen-year-olds no longer take themselves, or growing up, with the same diehard seriousness that they did at age thirteen.

Corresponding to the increased emotional maturity of the fourteen-year-old is a new degree of self-evaluation and self-acceptance. Although young people at this age still admire and want to be like certain idols, they also find much to like about themselves, both in appearance and in personality. They recognize as positive qualities within themselves, such traits as the ability to get along with people and a good sense of humor. Many also take pride in their ability to get good grades and in their athletic skill. But children of fourteen do not brag about themselves and dislike peers who do brag. On the whole, then, while fourteen-year-olds see room for improvement and change within themselves, they can accept themselves as they are with both their strengths and weaknesses.

Fourteen is also the age when friendships blossom out again, but on a new and different basis. Among fourteen-year-old girls the group, whether it be two or seven, becomes all-important. The bases of friendships have, however, now changed. It is no longer proximity or activities that form the bonds but rather interpersonal qualities such as "she is fun to be with" or "she is ladylike and kind." Fourteen-year-old girls do a lot of talking among themselves, and this talk often centers about the personalities of their friends and about social issues. In general, however, the discussions are fairly wide-ranging and include schoolwork and, inevitably, boys. Girls who are left out of these groups feel very lonely and often work very hard to be accepted.

Boys, too, show an increased friendliness at age fourteen, but they are more likely to be part of a loosely knit gang of boys than of a clique, the reverse of what holds for girls. Boys, too, begin to pick friends on the basis of personal qualities rather than activities, although they may be unaware of the reasons they befriend particular people. Boys have a lot of good-natured fun with their friends, and each group seems to have boys who fit into more or less stereotyped roles. Each group seems to have its comedian, its activity leader, its "brain," and its "Don Juan." These roles merely complement one another, so that by being in the group the boy can vicariously live each of these roles. There is a certain sympathy and compassion too, and boys who are left out are often given support by more popular or "in group" boys.

When we look at heterosexual relations, again there is considerable change from age thirteen. At age fourteen there is quite a good deal of interaction between boys and girls in socially acceptable and nonchildish activities such as parties, dances, and dates. Boys and girls now mix better and are better able to carry on a meaningful conversation. Today both boys and girls ask one another for dates. Fourteen-year-old girls also begin to be interested in older boys, who are more attuned to their own level of maturity. Fourteen-year-old boys are still likely to "horse around" a good deal at parties and dances, whereas older boys are more interested in dancing with and talking to girls. Dating is more frequent among girls than among boys at this age. Fourteen-year-old boys have to be in the "right mood," whereas the girl is likely to go on dates as often as she is asked and as frequently as parents permit.

One characteristic of fourteen-year-olds is the tendency to think and plan out their activities, not just for the moment, but for the whole year. They look forward to the different seasons and to the activities appropriate to each of these seasons. Boys are increasingly interested in sports, and the new strength and coordination present at age fourteen makes these activities more fun and more vigorous than before. Certain boys, moreover, begin to stand out with respect to athletic ability. Girls tend to be less interested in sports than boys and do not spontaneously organize games as boys do. They are more likely to participate in the sports that are sponsored by the school.

Perhaps the most important activity at age fourteen is socialization, and young people of this age spend the majority of their free time in social gatherings. The structure of these group gatherings is rather loose and free-floating, not unlike an adult cocktail party. In addition to these gatherings, much socializing goes on by way of the telephone, which is in almost constant use by the fourteen-year-old girl in particular. Boys use the phone, too, but their interest is now beginning to turn towards cars, and they experience a longing to drive and to own an automobile—a longing that will mount in intensity with each succeeding year.

The sociability of the fourteen-year-old is also apparent in the school setting, where he works well as a group member and takes pride in being part of a particular class. His greater self-acceptance leads to more respect for teachers, and his openness tends to make him an avid learner. His sociability, however, sometimes gets in the way, and he may be involved in so many extracurricular activities that his schoolwork does not receive sufficient attention. At this age, for example, a young person may become more involved in electing student officers and in student organizations than in school work proper.

The fourteen-year-old wants to learn on his own, to try out, and to explore. He can tolerate failure if it is not coupled with criticism. At this age he is particularly interested in social studies, local and national politics, and current events. He is concerned with the study of man and likes biology, physiology, and even psychology. In contrast to the thirteen-year-old, the young person at fourteen likes to express himself publicly by giving reports, engaging in public speaking and in dramatics. At this age, then, the adult's problem is to exercise restraint and to rein in and channel the fourteen-year-old's exuberance and energy into educationally productive activities.

The Fifteen-Year-Old

The exuberance and outgoingness of the fourteen-year-old gives way, in the following year, to a more somber, quiet demeanor. In a way, the fourteen-year-old celebrates the establishment of a personal self and self-acceptance that is the first stage towards true independence. At fifteen a new phase is begun that has to do with separation from parents and adults. The gloom and depression of young people at this age may reflect the awareness that childhood has gone and they are nearing adulthood; separation from parents, marriage, and family is no longer in the far distant future but is very near indeed.

Because of the contrast with the mood of the previous year this age has sometimes been called the fifteen-year slump. The withdrawal of the fifteen-year-old need not be physical as well as mental as it is at thirteen. At this age young people can withdraw into themselves even in the midst of a crowd of people. In addition to the frequent periods of low mood is a sort of apathy and lethargy that makes adults regard fifteen-year-olds as lazy and uncooperative. There are of course times when fifteen-year-olds come out of their slump and show their subtle and mature humor. They are, in general, more complex and difficult to fathom than they were the year before, when outgoing exuberance was the rule.

Fifteen-year-olds become rather guarded about themselves. While trying as hard as possible to understand themselves (they have discovered that self-control and self-knowledge are not as simple and as easily come by as they had imagined), they are relatively uncommunicative. When they do communicate, one can never be sure whether a story is true or whether it is a story concocted for the adult's benefit. They are concerned that others will know too much about them, read their inner thoughts, and judge them harshly. While wanting to make a good impression, they often create just the opposite.

At this age independence and liberty are often uppermost in the young person's mind. She is resentful of anything that she construes as infringing upon her freedom. Questions as to her whereabouts and actions are often dismissed with words like "out" or "for a ride." Her answers to questions about her activities are generally entirely unsatisfactory. The awareness of impending adulthood makes the fifteen-year-old impatient at times for grown-up prerogatives.

Related to the wish for independence and liberty is the desire for self-improvement. Fifteen is a period during which the youth may undertake rigid regimes of study, exercise, or diet. At the same time the fifteen-year-old is also thinking realistically about the future, of what college she wants to attend or vocation she wants to follow. Girls are also thinking about marriage and its many implications. They think of men in terms of personal qualities they would like and only secondarily in terms of looks, although they don't want a husband who is ugly or obnoxious. In a sense, then, the fifteen-year-old is projecting herself realistically into the future.

Most fifteen-year-olds tend to absent themself from the home a good deal and, insofar as possible, divorce themselves from family activities such as picnics or visits to friends. If forced to attend, they make their unhappiness apparent. Young people at this age want to stay away from home as much as possible and would be out every night if they were able. This fact, and their tendency to detach themselves from the family, is often a source of friction. Parents interpret this behavior as ingratitude and sense, not entirely without cause, that their fifteen-year-old offspring are embarrassed and ashamed of their parents. It can be, but is clearly not in all cases, a hectic period in family life.

Fifteen-year-old girls continue the trend away from close, personal, one-to-one friendships and move more in groups. They congregate where they can and the main activity is, as always, talk and more talk, often at a fairly loud pitch. Boys tend to group at this age, also, but their "gangs" tend to be larger and to be organized more about activities such as sports. Among boys there is a great deal of "helping" activity, with one boy helping another at his job, at his chores, or working on a car.

Heterosexual relationships at this age level tend to be more matter-of-fact, and there is a common "take it or leave it" attitude about heterosexual activities. Girls are still more interested in boys than the reverse, but there is not so much emphasis upon particular boys. Dating is common and double-dating is more usual than single dating. The subject of "making out" is a constant preoccupation, and there is a lot of talk about how much kissing and petting should take place. In like-sexed groups the merits of particular boys and girls as kissing partners is a popular topic of discussion. In general, fifteen-year-old youngsters sort of let things happen but also behave in ways that cause things to happen as they want them to.

In contrast to the wide-ranging activities and interests of the fourteen-year-old, fifteens are more narrow and restricted. They may engage in particular activities, such as listening to records or seeing movies, until they are satiated or even dis-gusted with the activity. It may be that this tendency to over-indulge can account for the frequent periods of relaxation and "resting up." While they can get involved in recreational activi-ties, fifteen-year-olds are not interested in taking lessons or im-proving special skills. The exception is boys' interest in cars, which can become all-consuming. Spectator interest is also tak-ing precedence over active participation for a great many ado-lescents at this age. Girls tend to be less active than boys and spend much time talking in groups, on the phone, or writing to friends and relatives. The social activities of getting together, dating, and meeting for Cokes take up a good deal of the aver-age fifteen-year-old's spare time.

The negative attitude that the fifteen-year-old expresses towards home and family is also directed towards the school. It is an age when criticism of the school and of teachers is very great, and teaching this age group is not easy. The group spirit that animated fourteen-year-olds is much less evident at fifteen, when informal groupings and meetings are preferred. Young people at this age like more fluidity in their social organization and are not excited about such things as electing or being a class officer.

At this age there is a very great concern with definitions, with being clear, and with details. Young people want to know where they stand on social, moral, and political issues, and they want to know where adults stand as well. Some of their criticism of the school stems from their feelings that teachers either do not know where they stand or are not committed to the positions that they take, whether in regard to smoking or to political action. Young people at this age want teachers who are enthusiastic about their subjects, who express opinions, and who are not threatened if a student challenges them. If a student likes a teacher she may become overidentified and imitate some of the teacher's habits and speech patterns, often without being aware of doing so.

The age of fifteen is thus critical in the school setting. If the leadership potential among these young people is capitalized upon and their sense of group spirit is brought into play, antipathy to school can be overcome. But if teachers allow the antipathies of this age group to dull their enthusiasm, and if they become angry and react with anger, they are likely to lose the group. The frequency of dropouts at age sixteen is often due, in part at least, to bad handling of young people in grade ten.

The Sixteen-Year-Old

There is a certain parallel between the age of sixteen and the age of ten in the sense that at both these periods young people attain an equilibrium among the physical, emotional, and social growth forces with which they have been contending. At age sixteen, for example, the sulkiness and low mood of the fifteen-year-old give way to a remarkably even disposition. The sixteen-year-old doesn't get mad the way he used to and is more receptive to constructive criticism, which he may take seriously. When he is hurt by the remarks of others, he tends to cover up his feelings and to wait for them to dissipate. With close friends, however, the sixteen-year-old will share his true feelings. In this regard he has become quite adult in handling his emotional life. By and large, he is less sensitive, happier, and more self-starting than he was at age fifteen. Balance and moderation rather than extremes and exaggerations characterize the emotional life of the sixteen-year-old.

A new equilibrium is also reflected in the sixteen-year-old's self-concept. His earlier concern with independence has given way to a sense of having "made it" and of autonomy with respect to parents and other adults. Fortunately, this new sense of independence is modulated by a new awareness of the relativity of independence and of the fact that personal happiness and social existence are based upon mutual dependencies. As a consequence of these developments, the sixteen-year-old is more sociable and outgoing than he was a year earlier. He is at ease now when he performs the social graces such as introducing his parents to friends, and social situations are less stressful and more fun than they were heretofore.

Just as the ten-year-old liked age ten best, so does the sixteen-year-old like his present age. While he recognizes and acknowledges his bad qualities as well as his good qualities, he is more accepting of both. Perhaps because of this new self-acceptance the sixteen-year-old is not as concerned about choosing his line of work or profession and is willing to wait and see how things turn out. The sixteen-year-old boy has more or less made up his mind about whether or not to go to college, and he concerns himself with choosing the college itself. For more and more young women also, college and careers are being given priority over marriage and family. Today, marriage is losing its significance as a symbol of a woman's success in life.

Adolescents at age sixteen show a greater equilibrium and sense of equality in relationships with adults than was true at earlier ages. Both parents and young people are more relaxed about a number of issues that were the basis of earlier conflicts and acrimony. Parents are less apt to worry about the hours at which their offspring return home, in part because sixteen-year-olds show more responsibility and will call if they expect to be later than they anticipated. In addition, however, the new sense of independence and of equality with parents means that young people no longer have to defy their parents in order to prove how independent they really are.

Young people at age sixteen are more accepting of their mothers than they were at earlier ages and appreciate that a mother's concerns are genuine and not just curiosity and prying. The situation is a little different with fathers. While sixteen-year-olds are more willing to accept their fathers as they are, they are still a little afraid to be entirely open with them. A girl who is dating a boy of another religious faith, for example, may try to keep this fact from her father for fear of upsetting him. Fathers, on their side, seem to be more accepting of sixteen-year-old behaviors, and while they may lecture their offspring, open conflict is less frequent than at earlier ages. By and large, the adolescent's new sense of adulthood allows him to better understand and appreciate his parents and to share confidences and discuss issues on a more or less equal footing.

Sibling relations are also improved when the young person is sixteen. To be sure, the sixteen-year-old is so busy with his friends, and so frequently away from home, that the improvement may be a function of diminished interaction. But that is not the whole story because the sixteen-year-old now enjoys the admiration of his younger siblings and begins to take a parental attitude towards them. Indeed, the sixteen-year-old may even intercede for his younger brother or sister and say such things as "Don't worry, Mom, he'll be okay. He knows what he is doing." With older siblings, the sixteen-year-old feels more comfortable and on a more equal footing than ever before. The squabbling of the earlier years gives way to interesting discussions and to the discovery of one another as individuals.

Outside the home sixteen-year-olds have plenty of friends and spend more time with friends than with family. Friendships are less superficial than at earlier ages, and now young people share confidences, discuss issues, and enjoy shared activities with their friends. Girls at this age are less preoccupied with boys than they were at earlier ages and are less concerned with a particular boy. They are likely to drop a boy quickly if he becomes too amorous. At this age girls begin to enjoy boys whom they can talk to, who understand them but in whom they may have no romantic interest. Sixteen-year-old boys are less advanced in this regard, and most if not all of their interactions with girls have romantic over- or undertones. A good many boys at sixteen like to "play the field" and are not very interested in going steady. Boys meet girls at dances or at informal parties in the home. Such parties are often initiated and hostessed by the girls. Both boys and girls of sixteen enjoy such parties where everyone knows everyone else, where the music is loud, and where different activities such as dancing, singing, and talking are all going on at once.

The interests and activities of the sixteen-year-old show the same equilibrium evident in other spheres of his life. Whether it is team sports, playing a musical instrument, or skiing, the young person has integrated these activities into his life-style. The sixteen-year-old usually has attained sufficient mastery to allow both his parents and himself to feel comfortable about, say, letting him use his own judgment as to what slopes and trails to ski. In addition, boys are beginning to be interested in jobs, particularly jobs in which they exercise their new strength or continuing interests. Some boys pursue their interest in cars by working in gas stations or their interest in music by working as clerks in record shops. Girls seem less interested in jobs than boys, perhaps because baby-sitting jobs are readily available, perhaps because they are just not interested in working at this age.

Television-watching is relatively infrequent at age sixteen, and though most young people express great interest in reading, little reading actually gets done. The exception is magazines, which young people read avidly. Boys are likely to read magazines having to do with "hot rods" or mechanics or science; while girls are likely to read magazines that deal with clothing, make-up, and diet and that include some romantic stories. For the most part, sixteen-year-olds are so busy socializing with their friends that there is little energy or time for such things as TV viewing, reading, or movie attendance.

For many sixteen-year-olds sixteen is a turning point in education. For those young people who are planning to go on to college, school becomes more interesting and they feel they get more out of it, perhaps because they are more willing to work and because they are at the peak of their intellectual powers. Other sixteen-year-olds find school dull and boring and drop out as soon as the legal requirements of age have been met. In many communities, school-work programs and better provisions for practical and manual training in such things as auto mechanics, computer programming, and nursing have helped to keep young people in school and to prepare them with useful and marketable skills.

In many ways, then, the sixteen-year-old is rather far along in his movement towards adulthood. He has attained all but an inch or two of his final stature and feels comfortable with his new body dimensions. The first novelty and fear of sexual feelings have passed and the young person feels in control of his impulses. He feels himself to be more or less an equal with parents, older siblings, and other adults, and can discuss issues and share activities on an equal footing. He will, of course, meet new problems, as well as old ones, as he continues to grow and mature, but he will meet them in adult fashion. For the sixteen-year-old, childhood is past without regrets, and the future beckons him with promise and excitement.

Index